Working with Political Science Research Methods

PROBLEMS AND EXERCISES

Janet Buttolph Johnson
University of Delaware

H. T. Reynolds
University of Delaware

CQ PRESS

A Division of Congressional Quarterly Inc.
Washington, D.C.

CQ Press
1255 22nd Street, N.W., Suite 400
Washington, D.C. 20037

(202) 729-1900; toll-free, 1-866-4CQ-PRESS (1-866-427-7737)

www.cqpress.com

Printed and bound in the United States of America

08 07 06 05 04   5 4 3 2 1

ISBN: 1-56802-928-4

Contents

CHAPTER 1
Introduction

Practice makes perfect.

The idea of research methods turns off some students who believe political science should deal with government, issues, and politics. That's an understandable but, we think, misguided reaction. Most political arguments sooner or later raise claims of fact, as when someone says, "We *should* renew the assault weapons ban because it *reduces* crime rates (i.e., *causes* crime to fall)." The first part of the statement takes a normative position (something ought to be done), whereas the second makes a factual claim; it states that one thing leads to another whether or not anyone wants it to be the case. The goal of our textbook *Political Science Research Methods* is to show you how those two types of assertions can be separated and how the latter can be demonstrated empirically. The goal of this workbook is to help you apply those cognitive skills.

At first sight, achieving these objectives may seem easy. And it is! But it also requires a degree of thought and care. Moreover, the best way to acquire the necessary skills is to practice actively and then practice some more. After all, no team would prepare for a game simply by reading a scouting report. But if you make an honest effort, we believe the process of verification can be fascinating as well as informative.

Most of the exercises in this workbook ask you to think before writing. But the thought process is typically straightforward and certainly does not require a strong mathematical aptitude. A thorough reading of the text and attention to class notes plus a dose of common sense should be adequate.

Note also that many questions call for judgment and explanation, because they do not necessarily have one "correct" answer. Unless it's based on a straightforward calculation or reading of a table, the assignment may ask you to think about a possible solution and to defend your choice.

The chapters in this workbook follow the chapters in the main text. That is, we have exercises for each chapter except the first and last. It is important to read a chapter in the text *before* starting to do an assignment. Many questions require you to integrate a chapter's different elements. Hence, you can't just try to look up something without grasping the subject matter as a whole.

We stress time and again in the workbook that orderly, step-by-step thought will help you avoid errors. If you are asked to make any calculations, you should do them neatly on a separate piece of paper that you can, if the instructor approves, turn in along with your answers. Here's a tip: your intermediate calculations or scrap work should be written in such a way that someone can reconstruct your thought processes. Figure 1-1 provides a simple example. It shows that the respondent first clarified the requested information and then performed the computation on a separate sheet of paper.

Figure 1-2 gives an example of someone using the workbook itself as a scratch pad and the ensuing confusion that often comes from sloppy writing and thinking. Note that some of the numbers were copied incorrectly and that the arithmetical operations are out of order. (The correct answer, by the way, is $28,650, not $24,150.)

The CD-ROM that accompanies this book contains all the "data" you need. When you are looking for a specific data set that is mentioned in the workbook, simply click on the appropriate folder. For instance, if you are looking for bes2001.dat, bes2001.por, or bescodebook.txt, open the folder called "BES Data" and you will find all three. It also has several surveys and tables that you can explore on your own with appropriate software. Once you learn how to use a program it is easy to explore a wide variety of hypotheses and problems. We hope you take advantage of the opportunity, because besides being intrinsically interesting, knowledge of research methods provides skills that will help you in other courses and even in many professions.

Have fun!

FIGURE 1-1

Be Organized and Neat

Party	Freq.
Democrat	200
Republican	150
Independent	100
None	50
Total	500

[Separate sheet of paper]

Percent = Number over total times 100.

200 Dems/500 = 2/5 = .4

.4 × 100 = 40%

Refer to the table above.
What percent of the sample are Democrats?   40%

FIGURE 1-2

Sloppiness Leads to Errors

What is the mean, or average, per capita income of the following six countries?   24,150

Luxembourg	$32,700
United States	31,500
Bermuda	30,000
Switzerland	26,400
Singapore	26,300
Hong Kong	25,000

144,900

$$\frac{144{,}900}{5 \quad 6} = 24{,}150$$

32,500 32,700

31,500

3,000

26,400

26,300

25,500 25,800 25,000

1,414,900

CHAPTER 2
Studying Politics Scientifically

In Chapter 2 we described the scientific method and argued that it underlies empirical political science research. We admitted that empiricism is not the only method of obtaining knowledge—there are others that lots of people fervently adhere to—and a case can be made against trying to study politics scientifically. (There are even huge disagreements about the definition and nature of the scientific method.) Nevertheless, this way of acquiring knowledge is so common that many social scientists take it for granted. And so do many "average" citizens. The problem is that scientific claims are sometimes difficult to distinguish from other kinds of statements. Nor is it always clear if and how empirical analysis can be applied to propositions stated in theoretical and practical terms. The following questions, problems, and assignments therefore offer a chance to think about the application of the empirical approach. It is important to note at the outset that not all the questions have one "right" answer. Many, in fact, require a lot of careful thought. And it is often necessary to redefine or clarify words or phrases, to look for hidden assumptions, and to consider whether or not statements can be "translated" into scientific terms.

When appropriate, write your answers or responses in the spaces provided in the workbook. Here is an important tip that will be helpful in any research methods or quantitative course:

- Write your answers on scrap paper.
- Answer all the required questions.
- Go back to the beginning and check and rewrite.
- Then fill in your answers in the workbook.

It is usually a mistake to use the workbook pages as a scratch pad for outlining your answers or for intermediate calculations.

Exercise 2-1. Make a list of the characteristics of scientific knowledge. Write them here for help with some of the following questions.

_____

_____

_____

_____

_____

_____

_____

_____

_____

Exercise 2-2. The chapter mentions several characteristics of scientific knowledge. It also warns about confusing "commonsense" and "casual" observations with verified or potentially verifiable claims. With these considerations in mind, which of these statements would you consider to be an empirical claim? Which are normative statements? Which are so ambiguous that it's hard to tell? Write your responses in the space provided below each statement and briefly explain your answer.

a. Al Gore received more popular votes in the 2000 presidential election than George W. Bush.

_____

_____

_____

_____

_____

b. The death penalty deters crime.

  _____

  _____

  _____

  _____

  _____

c. There will always be some people living in poverty no matter how hard government tries to eliminate it.

  _____

  _____

  _____

  _____

  _____

d. Thou shall not kill.

  _____

  _____

  _____

  _____

  _____

e. All people are created equal.

  _____

  _____

  _____

  _____

  _____

f. Catholics are more likely to vote than Protestants.

_____

_____

_____

_____

_____

g. People in the Middle East would be far better off if they lived under democratic governments.

_____

_____

_____

_____

_____

h. Access to health care is a fundamental right.

_____

_____

_____

_____

_____

i. Abortion is wrong.

_____

_____

_____

_____

_____

j. If the United States had not fought the war in Vietnam, the Soviet Union would probably still exist and be as threatening as ever.

———————————————————————————————

———————————————————————————————

———————————————————————————————

———————————————————————————————

———————————————————————————————

k. It doesn't make any sense to vote because so many ballots are cast in an election no single vote is going to make a difference in the outcome.

———————————————————————————————

———————————————————————————————

———————————————————————————————

———————————————————————————————

———————————————————————————————

l. Since a study of marijuana showed no "substantial, systematic effect" on the brain, laws against this drug should be repealed.[1]

———————————————————————————————

———————————————————————————————

———————————————————————————————

———————————————————————————————

———————————————————————————————

[1] The study was cited in Brian Vastag, "Medical Marijuana Center Opens Doors," *JAMA* 290 (August 20, 2003), 878.

m. "Criminals are motivated by self-preservation, and handguns can therefore be a deterrent."[2]

_____

_____

_____

_____

_____

Exercise 2-3. Look back at statements in b, f, k, l, and m in Exercise 2-2 above. Which are inductive? Which are deductive? Explain.

_____

_____

_____

_____

_____

Exercise 2-4. Many people make the claim, "You can't predict human behavior." In light of our discussion of the scientific approach to political science, do you find this claim valid?

___

[2] John R. Lott, *More Guns, Less Crime,* 2d ed. (Chicago: University of Chicago Press, 2000), 5.

As researchers, you will no doubt notice that it is important—and sometimes difficult—to learn to decode texts and other sources for testable propositions. As an example, consider the recent statement made by Gregg Easterbrook in an op-ed piece for the *New York Times*:

> Had federal gas taxes gone up 50 cents a gallon 10 years ago several things might not have happened.... The S.U.V. [sports utility vehicle] and pick-up truck craze would not have occurred or would be much less popular; highway deaths would have been fewer ...; greenhouse-gas emissions in this country would be lower; Persian Gulf states would have less influence on the global economy and less significance to American foreign policy...."[3]

Although Easterbrook discusses something that *did not* happen, and hence makes a claim that may not be testable in its entirety, his remark clearly contains several empirical implications that can be investigated. One of his assertions becomes easier to see if it is rewritten slightly: the higher the price of gasoline, the fewer the highway fatalities. Why? He doesn't say, but presumably it is because people will drive less miles at lower speeds and use public transportation more. Although it might not be feasible in a research methods course, you *could* check the veracity or likelihood of the claim by, say, comparing the highway fatality rate in countries or states with varying prices of gas. Presumably in places where gasoline prices are steep compared with some appropriate average we would find that citizens drive less and also that there are fewer highway deaths. Of course, it would be necessary to control for other factors, as we show in Chapters 3 and 13.

What makes this an interesting and challenging problem is that one could argue that even in the face of high fuel taxes Americans will drive as much as ever but will switch to smaller, *lighter* vehicles that are inherently less safe than gas guzzlers. So in the end fatalities might go up even if gas taxes increase. This particular case demonstrates that empirical analyses can be both critical to the resolution of public controversies and devilishly difficult to analyze. Other parts of Easterbrook's essay are also inherently empirical but probably harder to document. It would be difficult, but not impossible, for example, to study the foreign policy implications of America's dependence on petroleum imports.

The following exercise asks you to identify potentially empirically testable arguments, the first step towards carrying out an analysis.

---

[3] Gregg Easterbrook, "The 50¢-a-Gallon Solution," *New York Times*, May 25, 2004, 27.

Exercise 2-5.   For this exercise, read the first section of a current issue of a local newspaper. List one or two questions that arise from current events related there.

_____

_____

_____

_____

Which of these, if any, could be addressed or studied scientifically? Which would not lend themselves to scientific analysis? In a paragraph or two explain why or why not.

Exercise 2-6.   Below are excerpts from the U.S. Supreme Court's landmark decision *Brown v. Board of Education* (347 U.S. 483 [1954]). Perhaps one of the most monumental determinations in the Court's history, it overturned a previous decision, *Plessy v. Ferguson* (1896), that established the doctrine of "separate but equal" treatment of races. This principle legitimized racially segregated schools as long as the facilities were substantially equal. The *Brown* decision rejecting "separate but equal" relied not only on abstract legal and moral principles but on many empirical claims as well. Can you pick out the assertions that seem to be based on or could be tested by scientific analysis? There may be lots of such statements. Underline the empirical arguments. Circle the scientific or empirical claims. Surround normative ones with brackets.

In approaching this problem [the effects of segregated schools], we cannot turn the clock back to 1868, when the Amendment was adopted, or even to 1896, when *Plessy v. Ferguson* was written. We must consider public education in the light of its full development and its present place in American life throughout . . . the Nation. Only in this way can it be determined if segregation in public schools deprives these plaintiffs of the equal protection of the laws.

Today, education is perhaps the most important function of state and local governments. Compulsory school attendance laws and the great expenditures for education both demonstrate our recognition of the importance of education to our democratic society. It is required in the performance of our most basic public responsibilities, even service in the armed forces. It is the very foundation of good citizenship. Today it is a principal instrument in awakening the child to cultural values, in preparing him for later professional training, and in helping him to adjust normally to his environment. In these days, it is doubtful that any child may reasonably be expected to succeed in life if he is denied the opportunity of an education. Such an opportunity, where the state has undertaken to provide it, is a right which must be made available to all on equal terms.

We come then to the question presented: Does segregation of children in public schools solely on the basis of race, even though the physical facilities and other "tangible" factors may be equal, deprive the children of the minority group of equal educational opportunities? We believe that it does.

Segregation of white and colored children in public schools has a detrimental effect upon the colored children. The impact is greater when it has the sanction of the law, for the policy of separating the races is usually interpreted as denoting the inferiority of the negro group. A sense of inferiority affects the motivation of a child to learn. Segregation with the sanction of law, therefore, has a tendency to [retard] the educational and mental development of negro children and to deprive them of some of the benefits they would receive in a racial[ly] integrated school system.

We conclude that, in the field of public education, the doctrine of "separate but equal" has no place. Separate educational facilities are inherently unequal. Therefore, we hold that the plaintiffs and others similarly situated for whom the actions have been brought are, by reason of the segregation complained of, deprived of the equal protection of the laws guaranteed by the Fourteenth Amendment.

Now that you've located the case's empirical arguments, which do you think are the most important, and why?

_____

_____

_____

_____

_____

Exercise 2-7. Here is a statement made by Rep. Carolyn McCarthy (D-NY) on March 16, 2004. Subject her words to the same sort of analysis described in Exercise 2-6, underlining the empirical arguments, circling the scientific or empirical claims, and surrounding normative ones with brackets.

Mrs. McCARTHY of New York. Mr. Speaker, this past weekend Deputy Jason Scott of Tennessee was killed by a 16-year-old barricaded in his home with semi-automatic weapons with 30-round magazines. This must stop. One in five law enforcement officers slain in the line of duty is killed with an assault weapon. Our Nation's police officers have worked hard to keep assault weapons off our streets. That is why Congress must revisit the assault weapons ban without attaching special interest handouts. Otherwise, assault weapons will be back on our streets September 14. That is in 181 days. That is good news for terrorists, cop killers, drug dealers, and the terrorists that live among us here in our country. Unfortunately, it is bad news for America's families and police officers.

Since I took the floor a week ago tonight, over 400 Americans have died in this country from gun violence. But instead of the sense of urgency that we should do something about it, the House has stood idly by. Some seem content to let the assault weapons ban expire on September 13. The ban has kept us safer for the last 10 years. It has also respected the rights of gun owners, protecting the hunting rifles, shotguns and pistols favored by law-abiding citizens. Only criminals have been kept from their gun of choice. This explains why 66 percent of gun owners support renewing the ban. The American people support it by even more numbers.

Now that you've located the statement's empirical arguments, which do you think are the most important, and why?

_____

_____

_____

_____

_____

Exercise 2-8. Reread page 42 of the main text, especially the excerpt from David Easton's "The Current Meaning of Behavioralism." List the tenets of behavioral political science below.

_____

_____

_____

Exercise 2-9. "Traditional" political science was and continues to be criticized on several grounds. Make a list of them here.

_____

_____

_____

_____

DECODING THE AMBIGUITY OF POLITICAL DISCOURSE

As we stated above, political discourse is frequently ambiguous, and you have to think carefully about what words really say. Sometimes a politician's meaning is clear, as when the president says, "our country was attacked," which is a straightforward factual statement. But he also claims, "our military was not receiving the resources it needed." Certainly in President Bush's mind this too is a simple fact that could be empirically demonstrated. But the word "needed" in reality makes the statement a judgment, not a factual proposition. Whether something is needed or not is an opinion. In some people's mind the military has been receiving *more* than it needs, while others agree with the president that it has not. Who is right? It is hard to see how the proposition could be scientifically proven true or false.

Exercise 2-10. The accompanying CD contains a copy of a speech given by President George W. Bush to his supporters (look for "BushSupporterSpeech.doc" or "Bush SupporterSpeech.rtf"). Look for empirical generalizations, that is, statements that Bush intends to be taken as facts and not as his opinion. Which of those can you separate from normative assertions? Which statements purport to be factual or testable but are inherently nonempirical?

Exercise 2-11. For another case study, conduct a similar analysis on Sen. John Kerry's speech announcing his candidacy for president of the United States. That is, try to separate the "rhetorical chaff" from the truly "empirical wheat." It's available on the CD as "KerryCandidacySpeech.doc" and "KerryCandidacySpeech.rtf."

Exercise 2-12. One of the most important speeches of the Bush administration was his speech to the American people outlining the threat Iraq posed to world peace and security and why military intervention was likely to be the only possible response to the challenge. When reading this speech it is easy to delve into the pros and cons of the war in Iraq. But the task here is to sort through the various claims to see which are inherently verifiable and which are so ambiguous as to lie beyond scientific scrutiny. Doing so provides a good test of your understanding of the material in Chapter 2. Look for "BushIraqSpeech.doc" or "BushIraqSpeech.rtf."

Exercise 2-13. Among the complaints lodged against "traditional" political science were that it overemphasized law and values, that it rested on subjective observation, and that it described particular events or institutions rather than explained general behavior. To get a sense of how the study of a particular topic has changed over time, read the following articles: Philip Marshall Brown, "The Theory of the Independence and Equality of States," *American Journal of International Law* 9 (April 1915): 305-335, and Bruce Bueno de Mesquita, "An Expected Utility Theory of International Conflict," *American Political Science Review* 74 (December 1980): 917-931. Do these articles follow the evolution of traditional into behavioral political science? In what specific ways? Most important, do modern studies help you understand the issues better than the earlier ones? Which do you find most informative?

Exercise 2-14. As we noted in Chapter 2, some observers charge that the social sciences, especially in the past, have exhibited gender and ethnic biases. Look for an article on, say, political participation that was published before 1940. (Your library, for example, may have back issues of the *American Political Science Review* or *Political Science Quarterly* and certainly the electronic database www.jstor.org does. In either case you can search back nearly 100 years.) Do you see any perhaps subtle biases in how different people are treated?

Research Design

Chapter 3 has two major goals. The first is to emphasize the importance of thinking through a research question in order to find methods and data that will throw light on the issue. The second is to describe an "ideal" standard of evidence against which results can be judged and to suggest some ways that researchers can strive to reach that level of verification.

On the surface political scientists engage in all sorts of activities, few of which may look like causal analysis. But in that part of the discipline that thinks of itself as "scientific," a major goal—the Holy Grail, so to speak—is the search for verifiable causal relationships.

We began the chapter by showing what is necessary to demonstrate causality and how hard it is to do so. We also argued that the randomized experiment provides a model for supporting causal claims. Unfortunately, as powerful as they are, true experiments are neither feasible nor ethical in many research contexts. So we suggested alternative designs that might be called "approximations to experiments." By that phrase we mean procedures that accomplish very roughly the same things as random assignment of subjects, physical manipulation and control of the test factor and experimental environment, and direct observation of measurement of behavior. But they do so indirectly and most often with statistics.

Most of the assignments below call for serious thought rather than paper-and-pencil calculations. The purpose is to ensure that some of the basic ideas are clearly comprehended. We do not expect that most students will be able to design and carry out a major *empirical* research project. At the same time, it is important to understand how systematic and rigorous research proceeds.

Exercise 3-1.   Here are some statements, including a few that appeared in the exercises for Chapter 2. Identify whether the statement makes a causal attribution or claim, merely states an association, or is too indeterminate to tell and briefly explain your response.

a.   The death penalty deters crime.

_____

_____

b.   There will always be some people living in poverty no matter how hard government tries to eliminate it.

_____

_____

c.   Catholics are more likely to vote than Protestants.

_____

_____

d.   "Marriage matters because it helps produce children who grow up to become responsible citizens. . . . [S]ingle-parent households are far more likely to produce children . . . who are dropouts, drug users, or criminals."[1]

_____

_____

e.   "Show me a southerner, and I'll show you a political conservative."

_____

_____

---

[1] Letter to the *New York Times,* February 1, 2004, p. 10.

Now, indicate which of the statements above might involve a spurious or partially spurious correlation, and why.

_____

_____

_____

_____

_____

Exercise 3-2. Chapter 1 brings up an important point about the judicial system in the United States. Recall that Jeffrey A. Segal and Albert D. Cover in one study and Jeff Yates and Andrew Whitford in another looked at how or on what grounds Supreme Court justices decide cases.[2] In particular, they asked whether justices rendered opinions solely on the basis of legal precedents and the application of law or whether other factors entered into the process. In the space below, draw three different diagrams that represent causal, spurious, and alternative propositions about judicial decision making. Also give a short verbal explanation of what the diagrams mean.

THINK ABOUT THE QUESTION
You do not need to know much about the Supreme Court to complete this exercise. First, reread the section in Chapter 1 "A Look into Judicial Decision Making." Then, identify and list some of the variables or factors that are supposed to influence justices' opinions. (An obvious example is the degree to which a justice strictly adheres to legal principles. But the literature cited in that section mentions many others.) Finally, think about how these variables might be interconnected. Which of the connections would you call causal? Which spurious?

---

[2] Jeffrey A. Segal and Albert D. Cover, "Ideological Values and the Votes of U.S. Supreme Court Justices," *American Political Science Review* 83 (June 1989): 557–565; Jeff Yates and Andrew Whitford, "Presidential Power and the United States Supreme Court," *Political Research Quarterly* 51 (June 1998): 539–550.

Exercise 3-3.   Suppose you find that the more police officers cities hire, the higher the crime rates in those places. (You might indeed find such a relationship if you consulted, for example, census data.) Does this mean that it is safe to infer a causal connection between the presence of police and the number of crimes or is it a spurious relationship?

_____

What would explain this connection? Can you think of a specific factor that might account for it? Draw causal diagrams illustrating the different explanations.

Exercise 3-4. Make a list of the strengths and weaknesses of randomized controlled experiments.

a. Strengths:

_____

_____

_____

_____

_____

_____

b. Weaknesses:

_____

_____

_____

_____

_____

_____

Exercise 3-5. An investigator wants to know if repeated and prolonged exposure to "pro-life" videos changes opinions about abortion policy. He draws a *random* sample of 100 people from the community of Nowhere and assigns them to one of four groups: The first 25 men to appear are assigned to Group 1; the rest of the males are then placed in Group 2; the first 25 females are assigned to Group 3 and the remaining females go to Group 4. (Groups 2 and 4 may have unequal numbers, but just ignore this possibility when answering.) The "treatments" are then:

Group 1: Over a period of three days the 25 male participants view 4 hours of anti-abortion commercials.

Group 2: The remaining males watch 4 hours of automobile television advertisements and then go home.

Group 3: 25 females watch the same anti-abortion ads for the same period of time as the men but in a different location.

Group 4: The remaining females see 1 hour of automobile commercials and then go home.

The subjects' attitudes about abortion policy are measured at the time they are assigned to a group *and* one week after the last treatment has been administered. For the two experimental groups the measurements show a large decrease in support for any kind of legal abortion. The control subjects did not change their views very much.

After collecting and analyzing all the data, the researcher arrives at two conclusions: First, exposure to persuasive messages does change opinions. In this case, the ads made both men and women less likely to support abortion rights. Second, the effect of the messages is exactly the same for men and women.

What do you think of this research design? In particular, answer these questions:

a. Assume for a moment that the research design is sound. To what population, if any, can the results be generalized? (Write "yes" or "no" and a comment if you wish.)

  i. The people of Nowhere: ⎯⎯⎯⎯⎯⎯⎯⎯⎯⎯⎯⎯⎯⎯⎯⎯⎯⎯⎯

  ii. Only the men of Nowhere: ⎯⎯⎯⎯⎯⎯⎯⎯⎯⎯⎯⎯⎯⎯⎯⎯⎯⎯

  iii. Only those people with heavy exposure to anti-abortion ads: ⎯⎯⎯⎯⎯⎯⎯

  ⎯⎯⎯⎯⎯⎯⎯⎯⎯⎯⎯⎯⎯⎯⎯⎯⎯⎯⎯⎯⎯⎯⎯⎯⎯⎯

  iv. Men and women in the United States: ⎯⎯⎯⎯⎯⎯⎯⎯⎯⎯⎯⎯⎯⎯

b. What is external validity? Is it a problem in this research? Explain.

c. Now go back to the design. Is it sound? Which of these research standards and principles seem to be violated? Explain:

Random sampling:

_____

_____

_____

Creation of a control group:

_____

_____

_____

Demand characteristics:

_____

_____

_____

Experimental mortality:

_____

_____

_____

Exercise 3-6. The Supreme Court in its *Brown v. Board of Education* decision[3] asked (see Exercise 2-6):

> Does segregation of children in public schools solely on the basis of race, even though the physical facilities and other "tangible" factors may be equal, deprive the children of the minority group of equal educational opportunities? We believe that it does.

a. Describe a possible relationship between segregation and educational opportunities that appears to have concerned the Court.

_____

_____

_____

b. Is it a causal relationship?

_____

c. If the Court asked you to provide empirical evidence that segregation has a negative causal effect on educational outcomes, what research design would you propose? Why? In particular, explain the strengths and weaknesses of a controlled experiment. Would a field experiment be useful? What would be its advantages and disadvantages? What ethical issues would be involved?

---

[3] *Brown v. Board of Education* (347 U.S. 483 [1954]).

Exercise 3-7. This assignment will continue in Chapters 5, 11, and 12. By August 2003, after the conventional military phase of the war in Iraq was over, many commentators and political leaders, especially Democrats, began to express doubts about President George W. Bush's stated reasons for starting the conflict. They argued that the president misled the nation because no weapons of mass destruction had been found and there was no credible evidence linking the Iraqi regime to terrorist groups. It is natural to wonder whether these charges affected the president's approval ratings, and whether they decreased support for the war.

Suppose the White House asked you, as a research consultant, to answer these questions. The president's staff wants to know if all the widely expressed doubts about the war's justification are affecting the president's reelection chances. They are willing to fund your research but first need assurances that you can provide reliable and valid responses. You therefore need to decide upon a research design or strategy that would best suit the problem.

What you want to know is what happened to trends in opinions before and after the "intervention," that is, the emergence of criticisms of the president's reasons for going to war. Randomized experiments in which an investigator literally administers a test factor or stimulus are ideal for making inferences

EXPERIMENTS VERSUS NONEXPERIMENTS
Read the section of Chapter 3 entitled "Nonexperimental Time Series Design." (This topic is important in empirical research.) You might think of this problem as involving a before-and-after question. In other words, you might conceptualize the problem as in the following figure:

Before-and-After Study

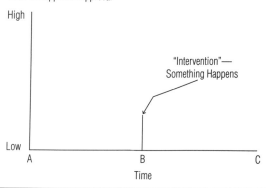

about the causal effects of interventions such as "new" knowledge on opinions. But clearly that strategy would not be feasible in this case. For one thing, the criticisms did not suddenly appear on one day. Still, you could pick a time after which they began to appear with great frequency.

In a brief response, answer the following questions: Could you make use of polling conducted by commercial and nonprofit organizations? How would you use that information? You might have to pick a time period that more or less demarcates the appearance of the intervention. What shortcomings would your design have? How could it be improved? You might also think about and identify some "quasi" experiment and control groups.

Exercise 3-8. Refer to Figure 3-9 of the textbook. Assume that you have used a "two-wave" panel design to measure the impact of media exposure on public opinion and that you knew when the White House media campaign was going to start. (Review pages 83–84 for our discussion of panel studies.)

a. At what point (A, B, or C) would you have conducted the first wave (taken the first measurements)?

_____

b. What would you have measured at this time?

_____

c. When could you have conducted the second wave?

_____

d. At what point would you be able to know who was in the quasi-control group and who was in the quasi-experimental group?

_____

e. What would you conclude? Did exposure to the media campaign have an effect on people's opinions on health care policy?

_____

Exercise 3-9. Consider this hypothetical research project: A pair of political scientists, working with a limited budget, want to determine if handing out campaign literature to people just before they enter the polling place will have any effect on voters. Consequently, they ask each person how he or she intends to vote and then give them a brochure to read. When the subjects leave they are asked how they voted. To control for demographic factors one investigator goes to a suburban voting station, the other to one located in an urban neighborhood. They report that on average the brochures increased the support for the designated candidate by 15 percent. Their final report claims that contacting voters just before they cast their votes could cause a substantial increase in a candidate's support.

In the space below, state the research hypothesis or question as clearly and succinctly as possible. Then evaluate the strengths and weaknesses of this research strategy. (Tip: For your own edification you might peek ahead to Chapter 7 in order to see what ethical issues might arise in this kind of research.)

Exercise 3-10. For each of the following research questions describe the design or strategy you would propose to investigate the issue. Note that although you do not have to conduct the investigation, you should make your design as practical and moral as possible. Devise a strategy that you feel would maximize the "scientific" payoff.

a. What was the reason for President George W. Bush's decision to go to war in Iraq in 2003?

_____

_____

_____

_____

_____

b. What are the social and political attitudes of the voters who supported the winner of the next presidential election?

_____

_____

_____

_____

_____

c. What are the effects of increasing unemployment rates on people's distrust of government and business?

_____

_____

_____

_____

_____

d. Why do some states have the death penalty whereas others do not?

_____

_____

_____

_____

e. What effect does a city's enactment of a strict curfew for teenagers have on the crime rate?

_____

_____

_____

_____

f. What is the effect of a 50¢-a-gallon increase in the price of gasoline on the use of public transportation?

_____

_____

_____

_____

g. What was the reaction of the leadership of the Mexican political party PRI, Partido de la Revolución Democrática, a major Mexican political party, to the passage of the North American Free Trade Agreement?

_____

_____

_____

_____

Exercise 3-11. In a research methods course it is difficult to create a simulation and study its various outcomes. However, many realistic games or simulations are available on the Internet. One particularly fascinating example is the "National Budget Simulation." Although this simulation may be artificial and perhaps has a liberal bias, we guarantee that this one is fun and informative.

Each January the president submits to Congress a budget for the next fiscal year and Congress has to respond to it by accepting or increasing or decreasing the different proposals. The Congressional Budget Office, the White House's Office of Management and Budget, and other organizations look at current spending and revenue totals and try to estimate the results of cuts and additions. Since so much rides on the outcome, it is a very serious and contentious process. By participating in this simulation you can get a flavor of this interesting and important decision-making process.

To make it realistic, assume that you are a responsible policymaker who has two goals: to manage the federal budget responsibly *and* to stay in office. Politicians, for example, often proclaim their intention to "rein in run-away government spending," cut taxes, and balance the budget, all at the same time. These promises have been front and center in American political discourse for the last fifty years. Yet, during the whole period the budget has been, with very few exceptions, out of balance (spending exceeded revenue), and many programs have either continued at roughly their same levels or increased. So what is the problem? That's what you can find out by using the budget simulation. Just remember: many government programs are lightning rods because they are so popular either with the public as a whole or with powerful groups. If you tamper seriously with them, you put your political career in jeopardy. Make your choices carefully.

1. Go to the National Budget Simulation at www.budgetsim.org/nbs/ and read the instructions and "How to Play the Game." You will probably want to read the other background material as well. It's very brief but informative. There are a couple of longer articles on budget deficits. Look for "Do Budget Deficits Matter?"
2. Participate in the Simulation: Click on "Play the Short Version." (The "Long Version" works the same way but allows the user to make more specific cuts or increases in spending categories.)
3. After you click on that link you will be taken to a page that lists about two dozen budget categories, such as "Military Spending," "Natural Resources and the Environment," "Social Security," and "Administration of Justice." You can click on each category to get more information.
4. Then use the pop-up menu next to each category to make a cut, increase, or hold spending level. The choices are limited, but you can still get an idea of what will happen to the budget and to your political fortunes if you make certain budget decisions. For example, try cutting just one program that you feel is wasteful. See what happens to the overall budget totals.

Suppose you think it's time to cut back on welfare spending, as many people do. In the pull-down list next to "Social Welfare Spending" click "cut 30%." This reduction, of course, is huge, and given the nature of American politics would be hard to get through Congress. Nevertheless, you can see how much it would help balance the budget. Keep everything else the same.

- Choose "cut 30%" for "Social Welfare Spending."
- Click "Find out what the budget is."
- Carefully read the top of the next page.

a. What is the current federal budget?

  _____

b. How much is the budget total after your cut?

  _____

c. What is the deficit?

  _____

Lower on the page you should see graphs that show how much money is spent on each budget category. By studying this information you should be able to see where the "real" savings can be found. The trouble is that those programs that consume the lion's share of federal funds are precisely the ones that are politically most popular.

d. Suppose you were a U.S. senator and proposed cutting Social Security by 20 percent? What would the new deficit be?

  _____

Try cutting or increasing a variety of programs to see if you can eliminate the budget deficit and remain in office. Or assume that you are advising a candidate running for the Senate. It is customary for candidates to propose a budget. Even though it has no chance of ever being enacted, the proposal points to the person's priorities and values. Assume that she asked you to prepare a realistic budget that reduces the deficit but does not alienate senior citizens, organized labor, environmentalists, veterans, farmers, and other groups in the state. Can you do it?

Besides spending programs, you can fiddle with tax cuts and so-called "tax expenditures." (Very briefly, if the government does not collect taxes because of tax exemptions such as interest payments on home mortgages the lost revenue has the same effect on the budget as if it were "spent" for some purpose.)

CHAPTER 4

The Building Blocks of Social Scientific Research:

Hypotheses, Concepts, and Variables

In Chapter 4 we explored some initial steps in the research process: how one may start with an interest in a political phenomenon or political concept, pose a research question about it, and propose an answer to the question in the form of a hypothesis. In this chapter we emphasize proposing suitable explanations for why a concept varies or how two concepts are related. A variable is a concept whose value is *not* constant; rather, it varies. Informed or suggested by theory or casual observation, hypotheses are *guesses* about relationships between variables. Hypotheses should be written so that the nature of the proposed relationship is clear, the concepts are distinct, and the unit of analysis is identi-

IDENTIFYING VARIABLES AND UNITS OF ANALYSIS
A hypothesis has three distinct and different components: the unit of analysis, the independent variable, and the dependent variable. Something cannot be both a unit of analysis and a variable. Something cannot be both an independent and a dependent variable.

fied. Concepts or variables are attributes of an entity, something or someone, which is called a unit of analysis. For example, units of analysis can be countries, cities, individuals, members of legislatures or courts, speeches, or government actions and activities.

Exercise 4-1. Which of the following research questions seeks to investigate a relationship between concepts? Rewrite each research question in the form of a hypothesis.

a. Do people's attitudes toward the environment vary by income?
b. What are the three environmental problems most frequently mentioned by high school students in South Africa?

Exercise 4-2. How could the following hypothesis be improved? First say how it could be improved, and then rewrite the hypothesis.

There is a correlation between intention to vote in 2004 and political satisfaction.

Exercise 4-3. For each cluster of variables, write three hypotheses. For each hypothesis identify the independent and dependent variables. What is the unit of analysis for each?

a. tone of campaign advertising
    closeness of election
    voter turnout

_____

_____

_____

_____

_____

_____

_____

_____

b. interest in politics
   perceived difference between major parties
   turning out to vote

_____

_____

_____

_____

_____

_____

_____

_____

_____

_____

Exercise 4-4. Listed below are five variables considered by Herrmann, Tetlock, and Visser in their research discussed in Chapter 1:

■ Isolationist/Internationalist Attitudes
■ Political Ideology
■ Military Assertiveness Attitudes
■ Willingness to Use Force (to defend attacked nation)
■ U.S. Interests (whether or not attacked nation involves U.S. interests)

Which of these variables is the dependent variable?

_____

Start to make an arrow diagram: place this variable in a box on the right-hand side of a piece of paper. Do you think that any of the remaining variables is/are likely to have occurred first, before the others? If so, place the variable(s) on the left side of your diagram. Are there any intervening variables? That is, of the remaining variables, are any of them influenced by the value of any of the left-most variable(s)? For each pair of variables, identify the independent variable and the dependent variable and write a hypothesis stating the expected relationship.

Exercise 4-5.   Below are sets of three variables. For each set, write a hypothesis relating the first two variables. Then state if and how you expect the third variable to affect the hypothesized relationship.

a.   concern for the environment
   participation in recycling program
   type of recycling program (curbside or drop-off)

_____

_____

_____

b.   gender
   perceived importance of workplace anti-harassment policies
   harassment experience

_____

_____

_____

CHAPTER 5

Conducting a Literature Review

Probably everyone would agree that picking and narrowing a topic is one of the hardest tasks confronting a new researcher. One can, of course, easily identify problem areas such as the "war on terror" or "the effects of television on democracy." But moving from a desire to "do something on . . ." to a specific theme that can be researched with relatively few resources and little time can be quite challenging.

Part of the difficulty lies in having enough information about the subject matter. What is already known about it? How have previous investigators studied it? What *important* questions remain unanswered? All these considerations motivate the "review of the literature."

In Chapter 2 of *Political Science Research Methods* we tried to provide readers with some insights and tips into conducting an effective literature review. But we attempted more. If a research topic can be stated precisely, half the battle is won. Thus, we also offered suggestions about limiting the scope of a project by examining previously conducted studies. We were particularly interested in making sure that everyone understood the differences between different kinds of sources, such as scholarly and mass circulation publications. We discussed the distinction between the search for literature—what someone else has said about something—and "raw" or "hard" data—information that is partially or totally unanalyzed. It is, for example, one thing to read a journalist's or scholar's account of public opinion polls. It is quite another to have the actual data so one can determine firsthand what they "say."

We assume that everyone knows roughly how to "surf" the Internet. So these assignments mainly force students to think carefully about what they are looking for and finding. As mentioned in the text book chapter, one can easily enough use Google or equivalent software to search for "terrorism" or "television" or any other subject. But these efforts are usually unsuccessful because they lead to too much irrelevant information. Hence, one will not get far with a mechanical machine hunt to construct a bibliography. Instead we encourage the application of more specialized databases and library tools.

Exercise 5-1.   Suppose you are working as a research assistant for a professor of political science who is beginning a new book about the "domestic consequences of globalization." She needs to make sure that she has read as much serious analytic writing as possible and wants you to begin compiling a bibliography of published materials. Which of these potential *hypothetical* sources would you add to the list? Why?

a.   An article in *Reader's Digest* entitled "I Lost My Job to a Nicaraguan."

_____

b.   An editorial in the *New York Times* called "The Bush Administration's Mistaken Trade Policy."

_____

c.   An article in the same paper headlined "Imports to the U.S. Soar."

_____

d.   An article in the *American Economic Review* on jobs lost to foreign trade.

_____

e.   An article in *Public Opinion Quarterly* on attitudes toward foreign countries.

_____

f.   An article in the same journal about changes in foreigners' attitudes toward the United States.

_____

g.   An article in the *American Political Science Review* on the World Trade Organization and Congress.

_____

h.   An article in *World Politics* about the emergence of China as a major oil importer.

_____

i. An article in *Newsweek* about the growth of the Internet in China.

    _____

j. An article in *Political Science Quarterly* about political party responses to foreign competition.

    _____

k. An article in *International Organization* about the ecological effects of international trade.

    _____

Exercise 5-2.   Suppose you want to write a term paper or scholarly report on one of the following subjects: "immigration," "nuclear nonproliferation treaty," "World Trade Organization," or "global warming." Use one of these popular search engines—Google, Alltheweb, or Yahoo—to begin building a bibliography.

a. Which search program did you choose? _____

b. How many "hits" did your first search produce?

    _____

c. How many on the *first* page of the search do you think would be helpful in writing an academic research report? Explain.

    _____

    _____

    _____

    _____

d. Properly cite the first source that you would consider using. See *Political Science Research Methods* for a suggested format.

    _____

    _____

e.   Now conduct a search using the remaining programs. Do these search engines generally locate the same sources, or are there important differences in what each finds?
Which do you prefer? Why? And, more important, do you see the need to limit a topic?

_____

_____

_____

_____

_____

_____

_____

_____

Exercise 5-3.   Chapter 1 included descriptions of several important substantive issues
in political science research. Use Jstor (www.Jstor.org), if available, or a library database
to compile a bibliography of *one* of the political scientists involved in those research programs. (Tip: it may be advantageous to pick the first author listed.) Record the author's
five most recent publications here:

Author's name: _____

1.   _____

_____

_____

_____

2.   _____

_____

_____

_____

3. _____

   _____

   _____

4. _____

   _____

   _____

5. _____

   _____

   _____

Exercise 5-4.   Pick one of the topics below. First compile a brief bibliography of three kinds of information about it: (1) articles in the mass media such as newspapers and magazines; (2) essays, reports, and discussions published on the Internet or elsewhere by advocacy groups, not-for-profit organizations, and government agencies; and (3) scholarly articles. This assignment requires familiarity with several types of literature reviews. Obviously the Internet provides a good starting place, especially for the first two types of information. But the third will require a visit to the campus library where the sorts of databases discussed in the chapter may in varying degrees be available. Naturally, you can use online resources as well. (See our discussion of "Jstor.")

SEARCH FOR AUTHORS' WEB PAGES
If you know of scholars who have conducted research on your topic—perhaps you have culled names from the bibliographies in textbooks—you can search for their Web pages. Frequently, they will provide a curriculum vitae or list of publications, some of which may be in electronic form.

Topics:

1. Do Harsh Penalties Have Any Effect on Illegal Drug Use?
2. Is the South More Politically Conservative than Other Regions?
3. European Public Opinion and the War in Iraq.
4. Why Some States Enact Laws against Gay Marriage.
5. Immigration to the United States from Latin America.

Using an acceptable format, list your sources here:

_____

_____

_____

_____

_____

_____

_____

_____

_____

_____

_____

_____

Exercise 5-5. The budget "simulation" assignment in Exercise 3-11 argued that cutting the federal budget is not easy because so many expensive programs are very popular with the public. The Internet address for that simulation is www.budgetsim.org/nbs/. If you did not participate in it or you do not recall the results, return to the simulation site, play the short version of the game, and look for the most expensive federal programs. Make a list of the top five here (the dollar amounts are not important, just the program names):

1. _____

2. _____

3. _____

4. _____

5. _____

Now, why is it hard to cut the federal budget, as so many politicians of both parties say they want to do? Try to find information that supports the argument that, although the public may not like government spending in the abstract, that same public nevertheless does favor maintaining or even increasing many costly *specific* programs. Can you find reports of polls that bolster this argument? Do any studies challenge it?

Optional. Would you like to try a more challenging assignment? Try to find actual data that can be reasonably easily analyzed. The Odom Center mentioned in the text chapter is one place to look. If you are able to access the data archive, you can find Lou Harris and other polls that should help you test the hypothesis. Another source is the General Social Survey (GSS). Search the Internet for "General Social Survey Home Page" or "Survey Documentation and Analysis." You should ultimately find a place that lets you directly analyze this massive, multiyear survey. It may take a while to get the hang of the facility, but once mastered it's an invaluable resource. The General Social Surveys are in a small way to social scientists what the Hubble Space Telescope is to astronomers and physicists, because it is used by so many public opinion analysts and statisticians. After locating a GSS home page, open a "codebook" or list of questions and browse for government programs, such as Social Security. You should then be able to find the percentage of respondents who over the years

PLACES TO LOOK

You might visit some of the opinion research institutes that are listed on the book's Web site. You can of course search for "public opinion and . . . ," where you substitute key words such as "government spending" or "social security." But be careful to note the sites' sponsors. Polls, as you may know, can be found to support almost any position. So, if a group or organization adamantly opposes a federal activity, its Web page may contain references to surveys that show opposition to the program. Therefore, a direct search of academic literature as in "Jstor" will perhaps be more rewarding.

have supported various programs. Alternatively, you can look at these percentages by year. To do so, go to the "frequencies/crosstabulation" page, enter "year" as the column variable, and the name of the spending variable in the row box. The results will be virtually self-explanatory.

A TRICK FOR FINDING SOURCES

Jstor may not be of much use because it does not yet archive many psychology journals where a lot of the relevant literature is published. Instead, try this tactic: use the Internet to find papers that take a position one way or the other. Then, as described in Chapter 5, consult the bibliographies and notes of the papers you find to "pyramid" further the list of sources. And, if in doubt about the references' appropriateness—are they based on sound research conducted by reputable scholars and organizations—try to track them down in the library.

Exercise 5-6. Suppose you are interning in a law firm. One of the partners tells you that the firm has taken on a client accused of selling pornographic magazines and videos. Part of the accusation is that obscene video, printed, and Internet materials encourage male aggressiveness and dehumanize potential victims. The defense will claim that there is little or no empirical research to support this particular aspect of the charge. Obviously she needs to justify this position and asks you to compile a list of scholarly research on the topic. It is important, she tells you, to find experimental or quasi-experimental studies conducted by independent authorities. It does not matter what the investigators find; all that is important is that results appear in scholarly literature. Moreover, her firm has already reviewed law journals and legal decisions. So you have to confine your investigation to social science (and possibly medical or health) sources. On a separate sheet list ten (10) of the reports you consider most relevant.

Exercise 5-7. In Chapter 3 we made the point that although experiments potentially have a high degree of internal validity they are not much used in political science. But they do appear as the main or subsidiary tool in many published papers. Sharpen your literature review skills by finding and listing six (6) articles that rely primarily or to some degree on randomized experiments. A specific database such as "Jstor" will be most rewarding. But here is a tip that can be applied to just about any kind of search: read *abstracts,* when available, instead of trying to skim entire articles. Using a correct format, list the results of your search here.

Exercise 5-8. An assignment in Chapter 3 asked how one might study the impact of the barrage of criticisms about President Bush's arguments for going to war with Iraq. One possibility was to examine trends in public opinion before and after the "intervention" (that is, the emergence of widespread criticism). Using the sources mentioned in Chapter 5 and on the *Political Science Research Methods* Web site, locate data that might be appropriate for a study of this kind.

To expedite your search keep three points in mind. First, you are being asked to search for actual data, numbers that can be downloaded or graphed and analyzed, or both. Look for numbers that you can manually copy, cut-and-paste into a worksheet or clipboard, or actually download. Articles *about* trends in opinion will not help you unless they are accompanied by time series data. Second, you will have to follow opinions about the president's popularity, job approval, and beliefs about and support for the war in Iraq. Do not get sidetracked by surveys on other topics, such as "If the election were held today, who would you vote for . . . ?" Third, think carefully about the analysis problem. Would, for example, a list of *yearly* average presidential approval ratings be useful? Or would it be better to collect monthly or weekly ratings?

CHAPTER 6

The Building Blocks of Social Scientific Research:

Measurement

Measurement involves deciding how to measure the presence, absence, or amount of the concepts that are the focus of your research project. Reliability and validity of measures are key concerns.

A reliable measure yields a consistent, stable result as long as the concept being measured remains unchanged. Measurement strategies that rely on people's memories, for example, may be quite unreliable, because their ability to remember specific information may vary, depending on when the measurement is made and the presence of distractions.

Valid measures correspond well with the meaning of the concept being measured. Researchers often develop rather elaborate schemes in order to measure complex concepts.

Level of measurement is an important aspect of a measurement scheme. There are four levels of measurement. Going from the lowest to the highest level, these are: nominal, ordinal, interval, and ratio. Choosing the appropriate statistics for the analysis of data depends on knowing the level of measurement of your variables. Frequently a variable

RECODING DATA
There are two strategies for recoding data to combine or collapse categories of a measure:
1. **Theoretical.** Choose categories that are meaningfully distinct, where theory would tell you that the differences between the categories are important or where you can see that there are distinct clusters of scores or values. For example, when combining actual household income amounts into income levels, a researcher might consider what the official poverty level is and group all households with incomes below that level into the lowest income group.
2. **Equally Sized Categories.** Choose categories so that each category has roughly an equal number of cases. In addition, limit the number of categories so that each category has at least ten cases.

can be measured using a variety of schemes. Choosing the scheme that uses the highest level possible provides the most information and is the most precise measure of a concept. Researchers frequently recode data, thus changing the level of measurement of a variable.

Exercise 6-1. What is the level of measurement of the following measures? If you think that the level of measurement could be more than one type, explain your choice.

a. Student major (arts and humanities, social sciences, natural sciences).

_____

b. Air quality (number of days air quality rated as good).

_____

c. Employment status (unemployed, hourly wage, salaried).

_____

d. Line item veto power (yes, no).

_____

e. Mental health insurance parity (parity not required, parity required).

_____

f. State income tax policy (no income tax, proportionate tax, graduated tax).

_____

g. Type of primary election (open, closed).

_____

h. Political party (Republican, Democratic, Green, Libertarian).

_____

i. Per capita foreign debt.

_____

j. Year of birth.

_____

k. Political ideology (strong conservative, conservative, neither conservative nor liberal, liberal, strong liberal).

_____

l. Type of recycling program (curbside pickup, drop-off).

_____

m. Age (18–25, 26–33, 34–44, 45–60, 60+).

_____

n. Type of housing (single family, semi-detached, multiple family).

_____

o. Zoning category (industrial, commercial, residential, agriculture).

_____

Exercise 6-2. Suppose you are studying the recycling participation rates of households living in a community in which there is weekly curbside pickup of recyclable materials. Which of the following questions do you think would give you the most reliable responses? Why?

a. How many weeks of the year during the past year did you put out recyclable materials to be picked up?
b. About how often do you put out material for recycling? More than half the time? About half of the time? Less than half the time?

Exercise 6-3. Herrmann, Tetlock, and Visser define the disposition of military assertiveness as "the inclination toward different methods of defending American interests abroad, in particular, whether a person prefers more militant and assertive strategies or more accommodative and cooperative approaches."[1] To measure military assertiveness, they used ten items. For the first eight items, they asked respondents to indicate whether they strongly agreed, agreed, neither agreed nor disagreed, disagreed, or strongly disagreed with the statement.

Which of the items below do you think are the most valid measures of the concept of "military assertiveness" and why? Which ones do you have trouble relating to the concept and why? What kind of validity (face or construct) do you think the items exhibit?

a. The best way to ensure world peace is through American military strength.
b. The use of military force only makes problems worse.
c. Rather than simply reacting to our enemies, it's better for us to strike first.
d. Generally, the more influence America has on other nations, the better off they are.
e. People can be divided into two distinct classes: the weak and the strong.
f. The facts on crime, sexual immorality, and the recent public disorders all show that we have to crack down harder on troublemakers if we are going to save our moral standards and preserve law and order.
g. Obedience and respect for authority are the most important virtues children should learn.
h. Although at times I may not agree with the government, my commitment to the United States always remains strong.
i. When you see the American flag flying, does it make you feel extremely good, somewhat good, or not very good?
j. How important is military defense spending to you personally: very important, important, or not at all important?

Most valid measures of the concept of "military assertiveness":

_____

_____

_____

_____

---

[1] Richard K. Herrmann, Philip E. Tetlock, and Penny S. Visser, "Mass Public Decisions to Go to War: A Cognitive-Interactionist Framework," *American Political Science Review* 93 (September 1999): 554.

Worst "fit" for concept?

_____

_____

_____

_____

Kind of validity?

_____

_____

_____

_____

Exercise 6-4. Which of the following goals would you consider liberal? conservative? neither?

a. Narrowing the gap between rich and poor.

_____

b. Encouraging belief in God.

_____

c. Promoting a modern scientific outlook.

_____

d. Protecting the rights of those accused of crime.

_____

e. Working for the rights of women.

_____

f. Preserving traditional family values.

    _____

g. Guaranteeing law and order in society.

    _____

h. Helping the economy grow.

    _____

i. Guaranteeing individual freedom.

    _____

j. Defending the community's standards of right and wrong.

    _____

k. Protecting the rights of individuals to live by any moral standards they choose.

    _____

Exercise 6-5. One strategy for measuring political ideology ("strategy 1") is to ask respondents how important each goal is to them, using the response scale of very important, somewhat important, neither important nor unimportant, somewhat unimportant, very unimportant. Answers could be scored and added together to create an index, with high scores indicating conservatism and low scores indicating liberalism. A second strategy ("strategy 2") is to ask respondents to choose between goals as in the following items:

a. Narrowing the gap between the rich and the poor or helping the economy grow?
b. Encouraging belief in God or promoting a modern scientific outlook?
c. Working for the rights of women or preserving traditional family values?
d. Guaranteeing law and order in society or guaranteeing individual freedom?
e. Being tougher on criminals or protecting the rights of those accused of crime?
f. Defending the community's standards of right and wrong or protecting the rights of individuals to live by any moral standard they choose?

For each pair of choices, one choice would be considered the liberal choice, the other the conservative choice. The total number of conservative choices could be calculated to produce a liberal-conservative index score.

Which of these strategies, 1 or 2, would be better at distinguishing between conservatives and liberals?

Exercise 6-6.   Table 6-1 below shows the distribution of senators' scores on the League of Conservation Voters (LCV) index. The scores range from 0 to 100 and represent the percentage of times that a senator voted in favor of the LCV position on selected issues. Suppose that you wanted to group the senators' scores into categories for a new variable called "Support for LCV." How many categories would you create? What range of values would be included in each of the categories? How would you label the categories? What level of measurement is the new variable?

TABLE 6-1
League of Conservation Voters Index Scores

Score		Frequency	Percent	Valid Percent	Cumulative Percent
Valid	0	13	12.5	13.0	13.0
	4	13	12.5	13.0	26.0
	8	9	8.7	9.0	35.0
	12	3	2.9	3.0	38.0
	16	2	1.9	2.0	40.0
	20	2	1.9	2.0	42.0
	24	1	1.0	1.0	43.0
	28	2	1.9	2.0	45.0
	32	1	1.0	1.0	46.0
	36	2	1.9	2.0	48.0
	44	1	1.0	1.0	49.0
	52	4	3.8	4.0	53.0
	56	5	4.8	5.0	58.0
	60	2	1.9	2.0	60.0
	64	5	4.8	5.0	65.0
	68	4	3.8	4.0	69.0
	72	3	2.9	3.0	72.0
	76	3	2.9	3.0	75.0
	80	7	6.7	7.0	82.0
	84	3	2.9	3.0	85.0
	88	3	2.9	3.0	88.0
	92	5	4.8	5.0	93.0
	96	5	4.8	5.0	98.0
	100	2	1.9	2.0	100.0
Total		100	96.2	100.0	

Exercise 6-7. Now look at the following table (Table 6-2), which contains a frequency distribution of senators' scores on the American Federation of Labor–Congress of Industrial Organizations (AFL–CIO) rating system. Are there natural clusters of scores? Where would you draw the dividing lines to reflect these clusters and to end up with the cases distributed roughly equally between three categories?

TABLE 6-2

AFL-CIO Rating System Scores

Score		Frequency	Percent	Valid Percent	Cumulative Percent
Valid	0	36	34.6	40.9	40.9
	13	5	4.8	5.7	46.6
	14	3	2.9	3.4	50.0
	25	2	1.9	2.3	52.3
	38	1	1.0	1.1	53.4
	50	6	5.8	6.8	60.2
	60	1	1.0	1.1	61.4
	63	6	5.8	6.8	68.2
	67	1	1.0	1.1	69.3
	71	2	1.9	2.3	71.6
	75	16	15.4	18.2	89.8
	80	1	1.0	1.1	90.9
	86	2	1.9	2.3	93.2
	88	6	5.8	6.8	100.0
Total		88	84.6	100.0	

CHAPTER 7

Making Empirical Observations: Direct and Indirect Observation

Observation of political activities and behaviors is a data collection method that can be used profitably by political scientists. Although some observation studies require a considerable amount of time and our presence in particular locations, most of us are likely to have used this method to learn about politics in a casual manner, without traveling great distances or staying in a setting for a long time. With some imagination, one can find numerous opportunities to use observa-

---

BE CAREFUL WHEN OBSERVING THE PUBLIC

In Chapter 7 we discuss several ways to make direct and indirect observations. In general, and especially, if you are working through a university or college, you must obtain the informed consent of individuals you question in a poll or survey or use in an experiment. Getting this agreement may be a straightforward matter of asking for permission, which subjects should feel completely free to give or deny. You may, however, be involved in direct or indirect observation of people (or their possessions) that does not involve face-to-face contact. (Suppose, for example, you want to observe a protest march.) Even in this case you should accept some standards of responsible and courteous research. If so, keep a few points in mind.

- Be aware of your personal safety. Make sure someone knows where you are going. Carry proper identification. It also wouldn't hurt to carry a letter of introduction from your professor, supervisor, or employer.
- Depending on the nature of the study, contact local authorities to tell them that you will be in a certain area collecting data in a particular way. If you seem to be just "hanging around" a neighborhood or park or schoolyard, you are inevitably going to be reported as "someone acting suspicious."
- Always ask permission if you enter private property. If no one is available to give it, come back later or try somewhere else. Even in many public accommodations such as arenas or department stores you will probably need to get prior approval to do your research.
- Respect people's privacy even when they are in public places.
- Do not misrepresent yourself. Here's what happened once to some of our students. They wanted to compare the treatment that whites and nonwhites received in rural welfare offices. But when applying for public assistance to observe the behavior of welfare officers by pretending to be needy they were actually breaking state and federal laws. They got off with a warning, but it's always a big mistake to fake being someone you're not just to collect data.
- Be willing, even eager, to share your results with those who have asked about your activities. Volunteer to send them a copy of your study. (Doing so will encourage cooperation.)
- When observing a demonstration, protest march, debate, or similar confrontation, do not appear to take sides.

---

tion systematically to collect information about political phenomena. For example, we can judge community concern about proposed school budgets by attending school board meetings. We can observe the nature of political comments made by those around us and how others react. We can assess power relationships or leadership styles by observing physical and verbal cues given by participants in various settings.

Exercise 7-1. David A. Bositis notes in his article on participant observation that "a key feature of participant observation design is an ability to both observe behavior and to provoke behaviors to be subsequently observed." [1] Reread Bositis's article and think of situations in which your participation (either your physical presence or verbal communications) could provoke behaviors to be observed. Are any ethical considerations raised by these situations? If not, think of a situation that poses some ethical issues. If the situations you thought of all pose ethical issues, try to think of one that does not raise ethical issues.

---

[1] David A. Bositis, "Some Observations on the Participant Method," *Political Behavior* 10 (Winter 1988): 338.

Exercise 7-2.   Read Laura Beth Nielsen's "Situating Legal Consciousness: Experiences and Attitudes of Ordinary Citizens about Law and Street Harassment" (*Law and Society Review* 34, no. 4 [2000]: 1055–1090), especially the "Method" section beginning on page 1061. How did observation play a role in her research? (You should be able to find this article in the library.)

Exercise 7-3.   Read James M. Glaser, "The Challenges of Campaign Watching: Seven Lessons of Participant-Observation Research" (*PS: Political Science and Politics* 29 [September 1996]: 533–537). Why is participant observation important to studying political campaigns? How important is flexibility in this type of research? (Available in Jstor.)

Exercise 7-4. Here are some ideas for collecting data and testing propositions with direct and indirect measurement. This list is suggestive. Obviously, you will have to modify the topics to suit your needs and interests.

a. Formulate a hypothesis about the behavior of members of your city council. (Example: in contentious debates Republican members appeal to patriotism more than Democrats.) After developing measures or indicators of this behavior, attend a public meeting or two to see if the hypothesis is supported. What did you find?

b. Think of a similar hypothesis for members of Congress and observe the floor or committee action of the Senate or House on CSPAN. Can you, for instance, show a systematic difference in the behavior of different party members or representatives from different regions of the country? Are the debates more courteous in one chamber than another?

c. Do you suppose there is an association between social and economic class and willingness to take a public stance on a controversial issue? Suppose in addition you want to observe what people actually do, not what they say they do, and you define "public stance" as displaying a politically based bumper sticker. Pick two nonpolitical events, one aimed at wealthy, educated individuals (an art museum opening, say) and another that might attract less educated, blue collar workers (a demolition derby perhaps). Count the number of "political" bumper stickers of the cars in the respective parking lots. Do the sample proportions differ? Is there a correlation between make and model and stands on issues?

CHAPTER 8

Document Analysis:
Using the Written Record

In Chapter 8 we discussed using the record-keeping activities of institutions, organizations, and individuals as sources of data for research projects. In some situations, as with the *Statistical Abstract of the United States* or the World Bank's *World Development Indicators,* the records will provide data that are directly usable as operational measures of concepts and variables, although you will need to decide how well these data measure the concepts you want to measure. In other cases, in order to create measures of your variables, you will need to analyze the records, using content analysis, for example. Much of the data you collect will be part of the "running" record, that is, collected on a routine basis by public organizations like the U.S. Census Bureau. It is less likely that you will use "episodic" records, that is, those records that are preserved in a casual, personal, and accidental manner.

Exercise 8-1.   Access the *Digest of Education Statistics* at http://nces.ed.gov/programs/digest/. Under the list of tables and figures, click on the year 2002. Under the items listed for chapter 1 you will find an entry for "Opinions on Education." Click on this and then click on table 23.

a.   What is the item in 2002 that was considered to be the most important problem facing local schools and what percentage of respondents chose this item?

_____

_____

_____

_____

b. How much has it changed over the years?

_____

_____

_____

_____

c. Where did the data for this table come from?

_____

_____

_____

_____

Exercise 8-2. Some of the data collected by the World Bank is available on its Web site, www.worldbank.org/data/wdi2004. Included on this site under "Primary Data Documentation" is a discussion of data accuracy issues. What are some of the sources of error in the data mentioned?

Exercise 8-3. Using the Web site mentioned in Exercise 8-2, choose "Environment" from the data menu. Here you will find a table on rural environment and land use that includes statistics on the average annual percentage of rural population growth between 1980 and 2002.

a. Which countries have the lowest growth rates?

_____

b. Which three countries have the highest growth rates?

_____

At the bottom of the table, this statistic is calculated for low-income, middle-income, and high-income countries.

c. What are the growth rates for the different income groups?

_____

d. What is the relationship between income and rural population growth?

_____

e. Which regions have the highest rates of rural population growth?

_____

In the folder, _Governors' State of the State Addresses_ on the CD ROM, you will find three governors' 2004 State of the State addresses. The first is from Alabama governor Bob Riley, the second from Arizona governor Janet Napolitano, and the third from New Hampshire governor Craig Benson. These were chosen to represent different regions of the country and to include both Democratic and Republican governors. (You can also find these addresses on the National Governors Association Web site at www.nga.org by clicking the link for "Governors" and then selecting "Governors' Speeches" from the bar on the left.)

In State of the State addresses, governors typically reflect on their accomplishments, identify problems needing state attention, present policy proposals, and establish themes and goals for the state during their administrations. Content analysis of these speeches should reveal similarities and differences among the states and governors.

Exercise 8-4.

a. Read each address and record in the chart below whether or not the themes or topics listed are present.

Topic/Theme	Alabama	Arizona	New Hampshire
Size of government			
Relations with federal government			
Relations with other states			
Bipartisanship			
Taxes			
Jobs, economic development			
Elementary and secondary education			
Higher education			
Health care			
Environment			
Budget			
Crime, prisons			
Drug use			
Mental health			
Homeland security			
Other policy topics			
Children			
Senior citizens			
Veterans, soldiers			
State employees			
Other population groups			

b. Which of the above categories need to be defined more clearly?

_____

_____

_____

c. If you had an entry for "other," how would you define it clearly so that it would be recognized in a speech?

_____

_____

_____

Exercise 8-5.   In this exercise you will evaluate the following ten paragraphs taken from Governor Napolitano's address:

Last year I reported to you that the state of the state was grim, and that we needed to get Arizona moving again. My friends, we are moving again. Our economy is starting to grow. For the first time in a long time, Arizonans believe the state is headed in the right direction. And there is an increasing sense of excitement about the future of the new Arizona.   [1]

I want to start with my efforts to help seniors combat spiraling prescription drug prices. Throughout last year, my administration built a prescription discount program that takes advantage of the purchasing power of Arizona's large senior population. The discounts we negotiated have saved disabled and senior Arizonans more than $1 million in less than seven months.   [2]

As we work to improve the lives of our senior population, we cannot forget the futures of our children. Arizona is internationally famous for its tourism attractions, its retirement communities, and its golf courses. Unfortunately, it is infamous for the number of children who live in poverty, start life without even basic immunization, and enter adulthood as high school dropouts.   [3]

In the new Arizona, young people themselves are recognizing the need to be immunized, and they are taking the initiative to educate their fellow students on the need to stay healthy through inoculation. One remarkable student joins us today. Jacob Anzar is a member of the Pascua Yaqui tribe and a senior at Phoenix's Genesis Academy. For nearly two years he has led a group of teens who   [4] have designed, written and produced an ad campaign to educate children on the importance of immunization. The student group, called Immunizers, is run entirely by students led by Jacob.

[5]   We need our children to be safe and healthy when they enter school, and we must provide them with an educational setting that prepares them for the 21st century economy. The business community has made very clear to me the best way I can help their businesses grow is to invest in a quality education system. We cannot simultaneously support the business community while opposing long-term investment in education. And true reform starts years before students enter the first grade.

[6]   Many other states cut funding to public universities and community colleges last year, but we did not. We recognize that higher education is the economic engine of the knowledge-based economy we are seeking to build in the new Arizona.

[7]   Trade with Mexico represents another tremendous opportunity to expand Arizona's economy. I have worked hard this year to enhance our already-strong relations with Mexico through productive meetings with Mexico President Vicente Fox and Sonora Governor Eduardo Bours.

[8]   The drought is still with us, along with overly dense forests being decimated by bark beetles. Our forests and the communities within them have never been so threatened.

[9]   Arizona is doing all it can to protect against the silent disaster of drought and beetle infestations, but the hard truth of the matter is that most of the forests that need treating are on federal land. And while Congress recently passed a forest health bill, it did so with inadequate funding and therefore no real promise of action.

[10]   We are able to do this, in part, because the efficiency of government has been greatly enhanced over the past year. My Efficiency Review team has worked with thousands of state employees to identify permanent savings and cost avoidances that will save the state at least $843 million over the next five years alone. I am pleased to submit a budget that will fund a leaner, smarter government for the new Arizona.

For each of these paragraphs identify the primary topic—the one given the most emphasis—by placing a check in the appropriate column in the chart below. In addition, decide whether the governor is mentioning the topic in a positive manner and as an achievement or if she is mentioning the topic in a negative manner and as a problem to be addressed. Record your evaluation in the tone column using a plus (+) or a minus (–) sign. After you have evaluated each paragraph, count the number of checks in each column. Write a short paragraph summarizing your results.

Paragraph	Budget/ Taxes	Education	Crime	Health Care	Economic Development	Environment	Other	Tone
1								
2								
3								
4								
5								
6								
7								
8								
9								
10								
Total								

Exercise 8-6. Using the kinds of techniques you've studied in the chapter and practiced above, compare the speeches of Republican and Democratic governors.

CHAPTER 9
Sampling

The attempt to verify statements empirically lies at the core of modern political science. Abstract theorizing is a valuable, even necessary, activity. Still, most social scientists feel that at some point theories have to "face reality." Thus, as we have seen in several chapters, carefully observing and collecting data is an integral part of the research process.

Unfortunately, in all too many situations it is not possible to observe each member of a population. Hence, sampling—the process of drawing a small set of cases from a larger population—becomes necessary.

The social sciences depend heavily on sampling. This fact sometimes troubles the general public. "How," many citizens ask, "can you make a claim about all the 290 million people in the United States when you've interviewed just 500 of them?" Still, some people, including many reporters, politicians, and political advisers, act as though polling is an exact science. The point of Chapter 9 is to address these issues.

More specifically, sampling raises two questions. First, *how* should the subset of observations be collected from the population, and second, *how reliable and valid* are inferences made on the basis of a sample? The first question pertains to sample types or designs, whereas the second deals with statistics and probability.

At this level of your training it is not possible to go into detail about either. But if you work through these assignments you may begin to get a feel for the ins and outs of sampling techniques and their properties. None of them involves any mathematical sophistication. But they do require careful thought.

Exercise 9-1. Refer again to Laura Beth Nielsen's article, "Situating Legal Consciousness: Experiences and Attitudes of Ordinary Citizens about Law and Street Harassment," [1] mentioned in Exercise 7-2, especially the "Method" section beginning on page 1061. Answer the following questions:

a. Did the author use a probability sample?

_____

_____

_____

_____

_____

b. How did the author select her sample?

_____

_____

_____

_____

_____

_____

_____

_____

_____

[1] Laura Beth Nielsen, "Situating Legal Consciousness: Experiences and Attitudes of Ordinary Citizens about Law and Street Harassment," *Law and Society Review* 34, no. 4 (2000): 1055–1090.

c. How did she try to limit bias in her sample?

_____

_____

_____

_____

_____

_____

_____

_____

d. How did the author's method of selecting her subjects ensure that they were appropriate for her study?

_____

_____

_____

_____

_____

_____

_____

_____

Exercise 9-2. Consider this hypothesis: High school students have political beliefs and attitudes similar to those of their parents. Both students and parents will be sent questionnaires and their responses compared. The work will be done at "South High," which has an enrollment of 2,000. Here are some ideas for collecting the data. In each instance identify the sampling "design" and indicate whether it would produce data for a satisfactory test of the hypothesis. Briefly explain. To what populations, if any, could the results be generalized? (Note: Do not worry about such aspects of the project as how questionnaires will be matched or obtaining permissions from the school board and others.)

a. Proposed sampling scheme: the investigator takes the first and last name (and address) from every other page of South High's student directory and mails a questionnaire to those students and their parents.

b. Proposed sampling scheme: beginning March 1 at 3:30, the investigator stands outside the entrance to South High and hands out questionnaires to passing students and asks that they and their parents return them.

c. Proposed sampling scheme: investigator asks South High's assistant principal to generate a random list of 200 student names and addresses. Each student and his or her parents are mailed a questionnaire.

_____

_____

_____

_____

_____

d. Proposed sampling scheme: the investigator asks the guidance counselor for the names of exactly 50 college-prep students, 50 general-study students, 50 vocational educational students, and 50 other students of any kind.

_____

_____

_____

_____

_____

e. Proposed sampling scheme: the investigator asks South High's assistant principal to draw (randomly) 50 names from each class (freshmen, sophomore, junior, and senior). Each student and his or her parents are mailed a questionnaire.

_____

_____

_____

_____

_____

Exercise 9-3. Suppose you work in the governor's office in Delaware. Newspapers have criticized the state government for not providing adequate services to ethnic minorities. You have been asked to compare the experiences of various ethnic groups with respect to treatment by public departments such as health, public safety, and education. You design a survey that among other things asks respondents to list their complaints about government programs. You will use the total number of grievances mentioned by each person as an indicator of his or her level of dissatisfaction. Now the question of sample size comes up. Your office has limited funds but needs to make reliable inferences. United States Bureau of the Census data indicate the population of Delaware is distributed as in the table below.[2] (Refer to pages 248–249 of the main text for an example.)

a. If you conduct a total simple random sample of 100, what is the expected number of people in each ethnic group? Round to the nearest whole number. Write them in the table.

b. What about a sample of 1,000? Enter these expectations in the last column.

c. Do you see any problems with the sample sizes? Explain.

_____

_____

_____

_____

_____

	Delaware Population, by Race, 2000		Expected Numbers for Samples of . . .	
Group	**Population**	**Percent**	**100**	**1,000**
White	584,773	77.79		
African American	150,666	20.04		
Asian	16,259	2.16		
Total	751,698	99.99		

---

[2] Source for this and next table: U.S. Bureau of the Census, *County and City Data Book, 2000*. Available on line at www.census.gov/statab/www/ccdb.html. Accessed July 5, 2004.

Exercise 9-4. Since you've done such a great job for Delaware, the governor of Vermont wants you to conduct similar research there. Census data for this state indicate the following population distribution.[3] (Refer to pages 248–249 of the main text for an example.)

a. If you conduct a total simple random sample of 100, what is the expected number of people in each ethnic group? Round to the nearest whole number. Enter the numbers in the appropriate column of the table.
b. What about a sample of 1,000? Place the numbers in the table's last column.
c. Is there a problem in this case? Explain.

_____

_____

_____

_____

_____

_____

_____

_____

_____

Group	Vermont Population, by Race, 2000 Population	Percent	Expected Numbers for Samples of . . . 100	1,000
White	589,208	98.61		
African American	3,063	.51		
Asian	5,217	.87		
Total	597,488	99.99		

---

[3] Ibid.

Exercise 9-5. To continue the previous case, suppose that to save money you collected a total sample of 100 *Vermonters*. But to make sure the ethnic groups were represented by adequate numbers you conducted a disproportionate sample and found the mean (average) number of complaints in each group. The sample sizes and average number of complaints per group are shown in the table.

a. What is the sampling fraction for each group? Write answers in the table. (Tip: ask what proportion of a group leads to a sample of 50 or 25, as the case may be.)

b. Suppose you found the sample mean (i.e., average) number of complaints for each ethnic group (see the table). For each ethnic group calculate its weighting factor that should enter the calculation of an overall estimate of the mean number of complaints. Put those numbers in the last columns. What is the *overall* weighted mean? (Tip: if the sample is disproportionate, members of some groups are by definition over-represented. So they should "count" for less when calculating the average. How did we do it in the text?)

Group	Final Sample Size	Average Number of Complaints	Sampling Fraction	Weighting Factor
Whites	50	1.0		
African Americans	25	4.5		
Asians	25	3.5		

Exercise 9-6. Below are some organizations and companies that do extensive polling. It is instructive to see how they conduct this research. It is especially interesting to compare not-for-profit or academic surveys with commercial polls. For each organization or company locate and identify the sample type and size they use in polling. Are there any differences between commercial and noncommercial surveys with regard to the types and sizes of samples used? (Note: By the time you read this some of the Internet addresses may have changed. But for the most part these are well-established programs and by searching for their names you should be able to locate the needed information quickly. You may have to use search features [described in Chapter 5] to find information on "how the polls are conducted.")

a.   Chicago Council on Foreign Affairs
     American Public Opinion and Foreign Policy
     www.worldviews.org/detailreports/usreport/index.htm

     Typical sample type (e.g., telephone, face-to-face): ————————————

     Typical sample size: ————————————————————

b.   National Opinion Research Center (NORC)
     General Social Surveys
     www.norc.org/projects/gensoc.asp

     Typical sample type (e.g., telephone, face-to-face): ————————————

     Typical sample size: ————————————————————

c.   National Election Studies (NES)
     www.umich.edu/~nes/

     Typical sample type (e.g., telephone, face-to-face): ————————————

     Typical sample size: ————————————————————

d.   The Pew Research Center
     http://people-press.org/

     Typical sample type (e.g., telephone, face-to-face): ————————————

     Typical sample size: ————————————————————

e. *Washington Post* Online
    www.washingtonpost.com/wp-srv/politics/polls/vault/vault.htm

    Typical sample type (e.g., telephone, face-to-face): _____

    Typical sample size: _____

f. *Los Angeles Times* Polls Index
    www.latimes.com

    Typical sample type (e.g., telephone, face-to-face): _____

    Typical sample size: _____

g. CBS News/*New York Times* Polls
    www.nytimes.com

    Typical sample type (e.g., telephone, face-to-face): _____

    Typical sample size: _____

h. *USA Today*
    www.usatoday.com/

    Typical sample type (e.g., telephone, face-to-face): _____

    Typical sample size: _____

i. As a rule do you see any noticeable differences in sampling methods and sizes?

    _____

    _____

    _____

    _____

    _____

    _____

    _____

    _____

Exercise 9-7. Health insurance is a major issue in American politics. According to the Census Bureau, the percentage of people in the United States without health insurance in 2002 was 15.2.[4] The consulting firm you work for doesn't completely trust this number and plans to conduct a survey on its own to check for itself. It asks you for some background information.

a. Assume .152 is the true proportion, P, of people not having health insurance. If you took a sample of 100 people living in the United States at that time, what would be the expected value of your estimator for this proportion? _____

b. Assume standard assumptions hold. What would be the standard error of this estimator? _____

c. Suppose the sample size were increased to 1,000. Now what is the expected value of your estimator? _____

d. What is the new standard error? _____

e. Explain to your employers in lay terms what the differences, if any, in the standard errors mean.

_____

_____

_____

_____

_____

_____

_____

_____

_____

_____

_____

_____

4. U.S. Bureau of the Census, "USA Statistics in Brief." Available online at www.census.gov/statab/www/part1.html. Accessed July 21, 2004.

UNDERSTANDING DATA FILES

Neither the textbook nor this workbook offers much instruction in using computer software to analyze data. That's because there are many software packages available and political scientists have not adopted a standard. So your instructor will have to guide your use of the program adopted for the course.

Nevertheless, most software works the same way, and we can provide a few general tips that may be helpful for getting data into a program such as SPSS.

File Extensions. First, be aware that information is stored electronically in different formats. You can often tell the format by looking at the file name and especially at the so-called *file extension,* the three letters after the period. Knowing the file format lets you pick the correct program or program options when reading or opening a data file. Some common types are:

.txt for "text" data or information. A text file contains just alphanumeric characters (e.g., letters, digits, punctuation marks, a few symbols), and when printed looks just like something created on a typewriter or simple printer. If a program "thinks" it's reading text data, it won't recognize hidden codes for different fonts, graphics, and so forth. Consequently, if your word processor or editor (e.g., NotePad) shows you a lot of gibberish, chances are that the file is not simple text. When you double click a filename of this sort your operating system's default word processor or editor will automatically try to open it. An example of a text file is "anes2000readme.txt," which describes a set of data pertaining to the 2000 American national election.

.dat for "data." The extension does indeed suggest data, but files of this type sometimes contain alphanumeric characters as well. In either case they can be loaded into a word processor. Moreover, some statistical programs recognize the "dat" extension as data and will try to open the data. SPSS, for example, reads these files. Go to "File," and then "Read text data." After locating the file in the menu box, the program will start a "Text Import Wizard," which takes you step by step through getting the data.[5] Examples of this format are "randomnumbers.dat," "surveytext.dat," and "surveydigits.dat." Depending on your system's configuration, double clicking on "dat" extension names will start a word processor or possibly a statistical program. But you can first run the program you want and then read the file.

.doc for "document" information. This extension usually means Microsoft Word–formatted information that contains hidden formatting codes and so forth. Unless you have changed options on your computer or do not have the Windows operating system, double clicking a "doc" file will start Microsoft Word. (As we mention in the text below, other word processors can open some versions of Word files, so you are not limited to just that particular package.)

---

f. Suppose a survey of 1,000 citizens finds that the proportion of respondents who report not having health insurance is .152. Would this sample result be unusual? Explain. (Tip: you might draw a very crude bar graph such as the textbook Figure 9-4, locate the *population* value under the peak bar, and then think about what the sample result suggests.)

_____

_____

_____

_____

_____

---

[5] At least version 11.0 of SPSS has this feature. Many other good program packages also have some equivalent facilities.

.sav and .por for SPSS data files. These file extensions "belong" to SPSS. Like most statistical program packages, this one allows you to give descriptive names to variables and their individual values and to create new variables or transform and recode variables in all sorts of ways. All this auxiliary information along with the raw data can then be saved in one file so it is available for reuse at a later time. The file extension "sav" stands for "saved." SPSS data and dictionary information can be saved in a slightly more general format called "por" for "portable." (We frequently use this option.) These files can be read by SPSS running on operating systems like Unix. An example is "surveydigits.por."

File Structure and Size. The file structure we use is quite simple: data are presented and stored in rectangular arrays in which each row represents a case (an individual, for instance), and the columns contain values of the variables. So if a file has 1,000 cases and 2 variables, the data structure is a 1,000-by-2 rectangular array of cells. Each cell holds a value for a specific case for a specific variable. (Note: To save space on the printed page we sometimes "unstacked" columns.) That is, the "surveydigits.dat" file, for example, actually has five columns of identification numbers and five columns of responses to make a 1,000-by-10-column matrix. But we arranged the numbers this way purely for convenience. Most software lets you stack columns on top of one another. Therefore, if you wanted, you could stack the columns 1, 3, 5, 7, and 9 of "surveydigits.dat" on top of each other and do the same with columns 2, 4, 6, 8, 10, to make a 5,000-by-2 array. Notice in addition that files with more than, say, 30 variables need more than one line when being printed on a monitor or average piece of paper. For these data sets the lines will "wrap" around making them difficult to read. Finally, if you are thinking about copying a file on a diskette, you can roughly estimate a file's size by multiplying the number of variables by the number of cases.

File delimiters. Most of the time the data points are separated by simple blank spaces. Occasionally, however, data are separated by "tabs." (In many systems the tab character is denoted by "^t"; that is, a caret and lower case t.) The 2000 American National Election Study mentioned in Exercise 9-12b, "anes2000.dat," has tabs for separators. Sometimes you have to keep this in mind when using certain software, but many times a program will detect the tabs automatically.

Case ID numbers. Note also that some data files have explicit identification numbers for each case (e.g., "surveytext.dat" and "surveydigits.dat). In others the case number is just the row number. When you view the data matrix in a program it will be clear which is the case.

Note: Our Web site (www.psrm.cqpress.com) contains all data files.

Exercise 9-8. The purpose of this and the following assignment is to illustrate sampling procedures and statistical estimation.

Assume that you have been asked by a nonprofit advocacy group with limited funds to conduct a simple poll. It wants to know the proportion of people in Dullsville, a town of 5,000 adults, that would oppose the establishment of a "halfway house" for women who have recently been released from prison. It believes that if 50 percent or fewer oppose the idea, it can begin negotiations with city officials on its creation. If, however, more than 50 percent are against the facility, the group may look for a site in another community.

Your task is to draw a random sample of 10 people from the population of residents and estimate the proportion that is against locating the facility in the community.

For this exercise you need two files from the CD-ROM, randomnumbers.dat (or .doc) and surveytext.dat (or .doc, or surveydigits.dat or .por): one contains a table of 10,000 random numbers. The other file is an enumeration of the "population." The 5,000 adults living in this community have been numbered consecutively from 1 to 5,000, and each person's response to a survey asking about the halfway house has been recorded as "For" (0) and "Against" (1) the proposal. In a nutshell, you will pick 10 numbers from the random number table and then locate those specific individuals in the survey file and record their responses. The proportion (or percent) of those in your sample who are against the house is your estimate of the population proportion.

By the way, your instructor knows the true value, P. This knowledge presents you with an interesting challenge, one that goes to the heart of statistical inference. If, like some students, you fall behind in your work, you might be tempted to "wing" this assignment by just making up and reporting a percentage without actually drawing a sample. The problem is that your guess has to be pretty good; otherwise, the instructor might infer that your estimate is *so far off the mark* that it couldn't have come from a truly random sample and that you must have cut corners. Suppose, for instance, your estimate of P is .1, whereas the true value is .8. This discrepancy might be grounds for doubting whether you did the work honestly. Still, and here is your problem, there is a chance, albeit very slight, that your sample result really does turn out to be .1, when the true value is actually .8. If you were "convicted" in this rare situation, the instructor would be making a mistake. Your knowledge of statistics may help you defend yourself.

In any event, to get you started, here are some more specific instructions. First, open the table of random numbers on the CD-ROM and copy it to your word-processing program. (You could print it out but there's no need to.) There are two formats for this file, a plain text version "randomnumbers.dat," which can be loaded into any program, such as Word, WordPad, or WordPerfect, and a second version stored in Microsoft Word format "randomnumbers.doc." [6] Whichever one you decide to use pick an arbitrary starting place in the table and copy 10 consecutive numbers in the spaces below. *Note, if you find a number larger than 5,000 (e.g., 6,889) just skip it and go to the next. These are your sample identification numbers.* Next, open the survey data file. It too comes in a couple of formats: "surveytext.dat" and "surveydigits.dat" are text files that can be read by most word processors. In the first the responses are recorded literally as "For" and "Against." The second codes the responses as 0 for "For" and 1 for "Against." (There is also a "portable" SPSS file, "surveydigits.por" that contains the numeric codes.)

Naturally, these files create an unrealistic situation. If you had the entire population's responses, you wouldn't need a sample. But let's pretend that the total population is inaccessible, as in real life, and that you can only draw a sample from it. So using either the text or digits file, search for the first respondent ID number and write his or her response in the table below. Then, locate the second person, record the answer, and continue until you have all 10 sample values. (Tip: let your program's "find" function help you locate the respondents. In most systems it is "control-F." Thus, if a number is 2,493, hit "control-F," enter "2,493," and press "OK." You should go right to that case. Note that if you are looking for individual 213, make sure you find "213" and not, say, "2,130."

---

[6] Several word processors will open files stored in a competitor's format. Hence, this version should be usable in many different situations. Example: recent versions of WordPerfect will read a Word .doc file.

a. Write the randomly chosen identification numbers and responses in the blank table below.

b. What is your estimate of the proportion *against* the halfway house?

_____

c. Write a one- or two-paragraph report for the group describing your results. Do you recommend going forward to the city council? Why? (Note: Reread the section "Sampling Distribution" in Chapter 9.)

_____

_____

_____

_____

_____

_____

_____

_____

_____

_____

Respondent Number	Response

Exercise 9-9. This assignment continues the previous one, but this time draw a *systematic* random sample of *10* identification numbers. (Reread the section on systematic samples in Chapter 9.)

a. For this situation you have to select every ————————————— observation (this is the sampling interval).

b. Choose a random starting point. What number did you get? (Note: If your start number is greater than 5,000, go to the next number or select another random starting place.)

——

c. Select the first case and record its response in the next table.

d. Draw 9 more cases by incrementing the previously selected number by the sample interval. Record the responses here. (Tip: after getting a starting number just keep adding the increment calculated in step a above to get the next number. Continue in this fashion until you are done. You don't literally have to count down the pages line by line until you get to the next number.)

e. For this sample, what is the estimated proportion against the proposed house?

——

Respondent Number	Response

f. Since both samples are random, combine the results to obtain an overall estimate of *P* and make a recommendation on that averaged value. Should the organization go ahead with its plans?

_____

_____

_____

_____

_____

_____

_____

_____

_____

_____

_____

_____

_____

_____

Exercise 9-10. Let's try to obtain an intuitive feel for sampling, estimation, and sampling distributions by drawing 10 more independent random samples from the population represented in the survey files and calculate a proportion for each. Load the file "survey digits.dat" into a statistical program that can draw random samples from rows. If you have access to SPSS, use the "surveydigits.por" file and open the data menu and click *Select Cases, Random sample of cases* to obtain samples from the columns. You will have to repeat this procedure ten times. Other programs allow you to copy a randomly selected set of row values into new columns. You need to do this 10 times to get 10 samples. Or, with a little bit of effort you can obtain the samples manually as you did in the previous exercises.

a. In any event, list the responses and estimated proportion of people against the halfway house in the table below.

b. What is the mean or average of these 10 sample proportions? _____

c. What statistical principle does this average illustrate?

_____

_____

Sample Number									
1	2	3	4	5	6	7	8	9	10

Exercise 9-11. If you were working for a nonprofit agency that is trying to encourage political mobilization in Africa, you might be asked to help plan and carry out surveys of citizens' attitudes toward participation and elections. At the moment the organization plans to conduct a study in a largely rural nation. There are no lists of voters. But a population census has recently been conducted and the numbers of people living in each province, district, and subdistrict are known to a reasonable degree of accuracy. Moreover, fairly detailed maps of these areas show detail down to block-sized segments. Given this information, propose a sampling strategy. Since the data are intended for statistical inference, you want the selection of people to be random. But of course a simple random sample is not possible. So what would you suggest as an alternative?

_____

_____

_____

_____

_____

_____

_____

_____

_____

_____

_____

_____

_____

_____

_____

_____

_____

Exercise 9-12. You can use the random numbers table discussed above to practice other sampling procedures.

a. Find a residential three-digit phone exchange in your community. (A phone directory should indicate which are residential exchanges.) Using the random number table, pick a random page, then a random column, and finally a random row. Use the first four digits on the line to complete the first of a random telephone number. Go to the second line and do the same thing. Repeat the process eight more times to create a sample of 10 randomly selected phone numbers. Write the numbers below. **Don't call any of these!** Instead, explain why this procedure might be better than using a systematic random sample of the directory itself.

_____

_____

_____

_____

_____

_____

_____

_____

_____

_____

b. Republicans have controlled the Congress of the United States since 1994. Suppose you wanted to estimate the public's level of satisfaction with that body's performance. Once again use the random numbers file to pick 10 random numbers between 1 and 1,807. (Remember: if a number is, say, 2,764, just skip it and go on.) Next, open the 2000 American National Election Study that is stored on the CD-ROM under the name "anes2000.dat" or "anes2000.por." *This time you will have to use a statistical program that can handle a large file because there are 1,807 cases and 71 variables. Using a word processor will be too much trouble. And note that the ".dat" file,* "anes2000.dat," *uses tab delimiters.* The guide or codebook for this data set is in a file called "anes2000readme.txt." It describes the variables (columns) and response codes.

   For this assignment don't worry about the weight variable or weighting the data. Find the first case in your sample and record the individual's answer to the question

"Do you approve or disapprove of the way the U.S. Congress has been handling its job?" (It's the 11th column, or the variable labeled "v000358" in the original study.) Do the same for the others in the sample and estimate the percentage of your 10 sample respondents who answer *either* "Approve strongly" or "Approve." Place the results in the table below.

Warning: some respondents will have so-called missing data, such as 8 for "don't know." Be sure to record these responses as well. But when calculating the percentages be sure to indicate if you used 10 in the numerator or just the number of non-missing responses. Suppose, for instance, 2 people strongly approve, 2 approve, 2 disapprove, 2 strongly disapprove, and 2 have "don't know" or "NA" scores. The percentage strongly approving is either 2/10 = 20 percent, or 2/8 = 25 percent, depending on whether the percentage is for the full *sample or only for those giving a "substantive" response. We take up this issue in greater detail in Chapter 11.*

Estimate percentage who approve strongly: —————————————————

	Respondent ID Number	Response
1		
2		
3		
4		
5		
6		
7		
8		
9		
10		

Elite Interviewing and Survey Research

The use of survey research and elite interviewing has become far more than a staple of empirical political science. These tools now guide decision-makers' thinking about public policy, appear as data in support of partisan arguments, and offer the mass media a way to inform their consumers about what is going on in the world. The reason is obvious: interviewing and polling supposedly provide objective "scientific" data. If, for example, a politician or organization can claim that more than half of the public favors a particular position, that stance might acquire a legitimacy it would not otherwise enjoy. So widespread is the use of polls to acquire information about what people think, they have now become part of everyday parlance of even apolitical citizens.

But as common and impressive as these methods are, they nevertheless need to be considered carefully. After all, everyone knows the adage "Ask a dumb question, get a dumb answer." It behooves students of politics to become familiar with what the techniques can and cannot accomplish.

Just as in the natural sciences, measuring and recording devices in the social sciences rest on theories. In surveying and elite interviewing the most fundamental premises are that respondents have certain information sought by the investigator, that they know how and are willing to provide it, and, perhaps most important, that everyone involved in the process shares to a high degree of approximation the meanings of the words and symbols employed in the information exchange. That is why Chapter 10 stresses the importance of thinking clearly about how questions are worded and presented to respondents, who may or may not care much about the researcher's topic. We note in particular that if questions are ambiguous or threatening, people may not answer them or answer them truthfully.

Please take some time to consider the assignments. They demand not only that you understand specific terms ("open-ended," for example) but also that you fully grasp the difficulty of designing an effective questionnaire, whether intended for an elite or mass audience.

Exercise 10-1. Suppose you are thinking of surveying the general public about "party identification," the psychological feeling of closeness or attachment to a political party. (Party identification is *not* party registration, which is a legal standing. It is an attitude or disposition toward a party.)

a. Write an example of a closed-ended question.

_____

_____

_____

_____

b. Write an example of an open-ended question.

_____

_____

_____

_____

c. Write an example of a reactive question.

_____

_____

_____

_____

d. Write a question that measures the *strength* or *intensity* of party identification. (Tip: see how major research organizations phrase such a question. Look on the Internet, for example, for "The NES Guide to Public Opinion and Political Behavior.")

_____

_____

_____

_____

Exercise 10-2. For each of the concepts or topics listed below, which would be most appropriate, a closed- or an open-ended question? Why? If either would be appropriate or possible, explain in sufficient detail to demonstrate your knowledge of the difference between the types of questions.

a. How a person voted in the last presidential election.

_____

_____

_____

_____

b. The reasons why President Bush decided to go to war with Iraq in 2003.

_____

_____

_____

_____

c. A person's trust in government.

_____

_____

_____

_____

d. A person's satisfaction with the criminal justice system in the United States.

_____

_____

_____

_____

e.   What a person likes or dislikes about the Democratic Party.

_____

_____

_____

_____

f.   A person's rating of a senator's performance in office.

_____

_____

_____

_____

g.   Support for a cut in the sales tax.

_____

_____

_____

_____

Exercise 10-3. Provide a short evaluation or critique of the following survey questions. If you do not see any problems, just say so.

a.   "What is your opinion of a national flat tax? Do you oppose or favor it, or don't you have an opinion?"

_____

_____

_____

_____

_____

b. "When talking with citizens we find that most of them oppose increasing the federal tax on gasoline. How about you? Would you favor or oppose an increase in the gasoline tax?"

_____

_____

_____

_____

_____

c. "Would you favor or oppose an increase in federal taxes on gasoline, even if it were a small one?"

_____

_____

_____

_____

_____

d. "In his statements about Iraq, do you think President Bush is telling the entire truth, mostly the truth but hiding something, or mostly lying?" [1]

_____

_____

_____

_____

_____

---

[1] *New York Times*/CBS News Poll, conducted June 23 through June 27, 2004, with 1,053 respondents. Cited in *New York Times*, June 29, 2004, 24.

Exercise 10-4. Suppose you are writing an article for your campus newspaper on the past session of the state legislature. A representative has agreed to a ten-minute interview. Which of these questions would be appropriate or inappropriate to ask? Briefly explain.

a. How many years have you been in the legislature?

_____

_____

_____

b. How did you vote on the bill to increase teachers' salaries?

_____

_____

_____

c. What do you think is the most important role for a legislator to play?

_____

_____

_____

d. What factors entered your decision to oppose the increase in teachers' salaries?

_____

_____

_____

e. What is your occupation?

_____

_____

_____

f. How did your training as a software engineer prepare you for the debate on increasing the sales tax?

_____

_____

_____

Exercise 10-5. Use the Internet to find several different polls of opinion on gun control. How were the questions worded? Which seems to you most balanced? Important: Do not get sidetracked on the merits of different positions. The point of this assignment is to see firsthand how question wording affects what we think we know about the public and how groups with a point of view rely on polling to support their positions.

Exercise 10-6. For which of the following situations would a randomized response technique be most appropriate? For which would this technique probably not be needed?

a. If a person reads a daily newspaper.

_____

_____

_____

_____

b. If a person has watched a pornographic videotape or DVD in the past six months.

_____

_____

_____

_____

c. If a person believes the Bible is the literal word of God.

_____

_____

_____

_____

d. If a person supports legalized abortion.

_____

_____

_____

_____

e. If a person has ever smoked marijuana.

_____

_____

_____

_____

f. If a person has smoked marijuana in the last month.

_____

_____

_____

_____

g. If a person has ever wished harm would befall a president of the United States.

_____

_____

_____

_____

CHAPTER 11

Univariate Data Analysis
and Descriptive Statistics

Chapter 11 begins the study of applied statistical analysis. Its main goal is to introduce in a nontechnical, nonthreatening way some tools to summarize a batch of numbers and make inferences. Besides being part and parcel of all fields of political science, many of these concepts appear in the mass media. Furthermore, political science leads to quite a few interesting and exciting career opportunities, but most of them require at least a rudimentary knowledge of quantitative research methods. Think, for example, of someone playing a major role in an election campaign. In all likelihood, she or he will have to analyze poll data or at least interpret and critique someone else's analysis. Or suppose you have an internship in a government agency. You may be of greater assistance to your employers if you can provide a modest amount of technical advice about reports they are receiving or advice the agency supplies the public. So there are lots of reasons for studying at least a few quantitative methods, no matter how far removed from the world of politics they seem to be.

Many students are initially put off by having to learn statistics, but our experience tells us that this aversion often results from unfamiliarity with the subject, not its inherent difficulty. So even if you are one who says, "I stink at math," at least attempt to keep an open mind. We think you may find that your anxieties are misplaced.

Here are a few tips:

- **Keep up.** Unlike some subjects that may seem to lend themselves to cramming, statistics is best learned step-by-step; you should make sure you understand each concept reasonably well before moving on to the next one. And since the ideas are possibly daunting at first sight, it is easy to get lost if you try to learn everything all at once. This is, in short, one course where it pays to stay on top of the readings and assignments.

- **Learn by doing.** You can't get into good physical shape by reading articles on conditioning. You have to go to the gym regularly. In the same way and for essentially the same reasons data analysis has to be learned actively. It is crucial that you *perform* your own analysis. Simply reading about how it is done will not give you the functional understanding that makes statistics so useful. The exercises in this book are designed to do just that: give you actual training in data analysis.

- **Keep substance over method.** Whenever possible think about the actual substantive context of a problem. You may be asked to calculate a mean or standard deviation, for example. But what is important is not the numbers per se, although they do have to be correct, but rather what they say about an actual problem. So instead of just writing, "the average is 10," say, "the average is 10 thousand dollars" in order to keep firmly in mind that you are working on a concrete issue and not some abstract algebra problem.

- **Be neat and orderly.** Yes, this advice sounds peevish. Yet we have found that a huge number of mistakes and misconceptions arise simply from disorderly note taking and hand calculations. It is always a good idea to have plenty of scrap paper handy and to work in a top-down fashion rather than jump all around the page putting intermediate calculations here and there in no logical order. It should be possible for you or anyone else to reconstruct your thought processes by following your calculations from beginning to end. That way errors and misunderstandings can be spotted and corrected.

- **Don't trust the computer.** Many of the questions we ask can be answered only with the assistance of a computer. And we are the first to admit that these are marvelous devices. But they have no ability to grasp what you mean to type and do not have the commonsense to decipher what to you may be obvious. (We have stressed in the text on several occasions that a computer can only do what it is told and consequently will not make a mistake unless directed to do so.) So every time you turn on the monitor be prepared. Ahead of time ask yourself, "What do I need to find out? What procedure will give me the answers?" If you find yourself getting frustrated or something will not "work" no matter how many times you try, back off. Turn the machine off, go for a brief walk, rewrite your questions on a fresh piece of paper, and then go back to the system.

In these assignments we ask you to examine one variable at a time. The idea is to summarize a possibly large batch of numbers with a few indicators of a distribution's central tendency, variation, and shape.

Exercise 11-1. Here are some variables that might arise in political research. For each one say what would be an appropriate measure of central tendency: the mean, the mode, or the median. If more than one seems useful, explain why.

a. A three-point scale of "level of trust in government."

    _____

    _____

b. The per capita incomes of the nations of North, Central, and South America.

    _____

    _____

c. The amount (in thousands of dollars) that a random sample of 500 New Yorkers contributed to the two major political parties in 2004.

    _____

    _____

d. The number of political activities a sample of 900 Europeans engaged in over the last two years.

    _____

    _____

e. The number of times Supreme Court justices voted to overturn an act of Congress during President Clinton's eight years in office.

    _____

    _____

f. Party identification in Great Britain.

    _____

    _____

Exercise 11-2. Table 11-1 contains some data that might come up in a discussion of gun control.

a. What is the mean death rate from firearms? _____

b. What is the median death rate? _____

c. Comment on the difference between the median and mean in this context.

_____

_____

_____

d. What is the maximum rate? _____

The minimum? _____

e. What is the simple sum of the deviations from the mean? (Tip: you don't need a calculator for this one.) _____

f. What is the sum of the absolute values of the deviations? _____

g. What is the mean deviation? _____

h. What is the total sum of squares (TSS)? _____

i. What is the standard deviation? _____

j. What is the variance of the death rates? _____

k. Draw a rough histogram or some other graphical device to describe the shape of the distribution. (You can probably determine this by using some of the quantities calculated above.) How would you describe the distribution's shape?

TABLE 11-1
Death Rates from Firearms Injuries, Selected Countries

Country	Death Rate from Firearms[a]
United States	13.7
Australia	2.9
Canada	3.9
Denmark	2.1
England and Wales	.4
France	6.3
Israel	2.8
Netherlands	.5
New Zealand	3.1
Norway	4.3
Scotland	.6

Source: U.S. Bureau of the Census, *Statistical Abstract of the United States: 1999,* 119th ed. (Washington, D.C., 1999), 837.

[a] Deaths per 100,000 population.

Exercise 11-3. Your opponent in a debate claims that for the last ten years the economic well-being of an ethnic group, A, has improved relative to the majority population. To support this claim she says *both* the mean and median household incomes are about the same. Yet can you imagine a situation in which the economic hardship of A is in some sense greater than the general population's? (Tip: what else besides central tendency tells you something about a distribution?)

Exercise 11-4. Table 11-2 contains data for twenty-three counties in Maryland. You should be able to perform most of the calculations requested below with a good calculator. (Tip: the kind of calculator that banks give away probably will not be much help. As described in the text, you need one that "accumulates" totals. Ask for a simple *statistical* calculator. You should be able to find a relatively inexpensive one.) Your instructor may, however, suggest or require that you use a statistical program package. A simple "plain" text-formatted version of these data is included in the data folder of the CD-ROM that accompanies this workbook. The file name is "marylandcounty.dat." (Save the data for future reference.)

TABLE 11-2

Social, Economic, and Political Indicators for Twenty-three Maryland Counties

County	Poverty Rate[a]	Crime Rate[b]	Per Capita Income[c]	Taxes per Capita[d]	Infant Death Rate[e]	Water Use[f]
Allegany	24.2	3311	20429	706	*	8
Anne Arundel	09.7	4457	30827	1222	07.4	7
Baltimore	12.8	4982	32269	1208	08.3	42
Calvert	10.4	2315	27063	1271	03.2	17
Caroline	20.4	3845	18375	708	16.4	17
Carroll	07.2	2237	27389	1038	06.7	3
Cecil	14.2	3569	24646	886	12.7	2
Charles	12.2	3699	26725	976	04.5	12
Dorchester	25.3	3931	20766	843	02.7	14
Frederick	08.6	2531	30021	1056	05.5	5
Garrett	24.2	1756	18293	914	08.9	1
Harford	09.6	2516	26613	973	05.7	3
Howard	06.6	3264	36294	1434	06.7	3
Kent	17.1	1931	26128	1033	*	4
Montgomery	08.8	3217	42393	1812	06.2	14
Prince Georges	15.1	6257	27996	1094	12.5	27
Queen Annes	11.3	3056	26878	1153	13.9	10
St. Marys	13.2	2387	27354	824	09.7	1
Somerset	29.1	3400	16006	479	08.5	3
Talbot	16.7	3438	32754	1192	03.1	2
Washington	15.7	2571	23282	817	04.5	4
Wicomico	21.6	5278	22929	895	03.7	9
Worcester	21.8	6168	25109	1963	12.1	4

Source: Bureau of the Census, *City and County Data Book, 2000.* Available online at http://www.census.gov/statab/www/ccdb.html. Accessed July 10, 2004.

Note: Asterisk denotes missing data.

[a] Percent of persons under eighteen below the poverty rate, 1997.
[b] Serious crime rate per 100,000 resident population, 1999.
[c] Per capita income, 1998.
[d] Local government revenue, taxes per capita, 1997.
[e] Infant deaths per 1,000 live births, 1997.
[f] Consumptive water use, millions of gallons per day.

a. The information in the table pertains to what kind of unit of analysis and hence is an example of what kind of data?

    _____

    _____

b. What are the mean, median, mode, range, standard deviation, and variance of water use?

    Mean: _____

    Median: _____

    Mode: _____

    Range: _____

    Standard deviation: _____

    Variance: _____

c. What are the mean, median, range, standard deviation, and variance of infant deaths? *Note: For this variable two observations are missing.*

    Mean: _____

    Median: _____

    Range: _____

    Standard deviation: _____

    Variance: _____

d. What is the approximate shape (i.e. normal or skewed) of the distribution of each of these variables?

    Crime rate: _____

    Per capita income: _____

    Water use: _____

    Poverty: _____

e. What is the interquartile range of these variables:

Tax rate: _____

Crime rate: _____

Exercise 11-5. During the course of the 2004 presidential campaign there was a lot of discussion about who benefited from the tax cuts initiated and signed into law by the Bush administration. If you refer to the campaign speeches on the book's CD-ROM (see, for instance, the assignments in Chapter 3) you will find that Sen. John Kerry said, "George Bush's only economic plan is lavish tax breaks for those at the top." Meanwhile, you will also find that the president proudly asserted, "I have twice led the United States Congress to pass historic tax relief for the American people." Part of the argument turned on dollar amounts received by different groups. A White House news release claimed, "Under the President's proposal to speed up tax relief, 92 million taxpayers would receive, on average, a tax cut of $1,083 in 2003."[1] Yet one of the president's critics wrote "the average working family would get about $289."[2] Assuming both sides are telling the truth, how do you suppose they could reach such different conclusions? You will not be able to answer definitively, but your knowledge of summary statistics should give you a good idea.

_____

_____

_____

_____

_____

_____

_____

_____

_____

_____

_____

[1] "The White House, Jobs and Economic Growth." Available online at www.whitehouse.gov/news/releases/2003/01/20030107.html. Accessed July 11, 2004.
[2] Kathryn Casa, "The Elephant in the Room," *CounterPunch*, edited by Alexander Cockburn and Jeffrey St. Clair. Available online at www.counterpunch.org/casa01292003.html. Accessed July 11, 2004.

Exercise 11-6. Consider this frequency distribution of party identification among members of a sample of the British electorate.

a. Fill in all the missing entries in the table.

b. What is the mode for these data? _____

Party	Frequency	Percent of Total	Percent of "Valid"
None	384		
Labour	1328		
Conservative	730		
Liberal Democrat	329		
Other party	126		
Missing	130		—
Totals	3027		

Source: David Sanders, Paul Whiteley, Harold Clarke, and Marianne Stewart, "British Election Study 2001/02," Economic and Social Research Council, University of Essex, Colchester, UK.

Note: Postelection study frequencies weighted by variable "postoctw."

Exercise 11-7. The CD-ROM contains two copies of a very small portion of the "British Election Study 2001/02" that was used in Exercise 11-6 above. One is in an SPSS portable document format, "bes2001.por," and the other in a plain text format, "bes2001.dat." The description of the variables is in a file called "bescodebook.txt," which is a plain text file that can be opened with just about any word processor. If you have access to the appropriate software, try performing these analyses:

a.   Create frequency distributions for "Your financial situation" ("Economic evaluation—self") and "the Nation's financial situation" ("Economic evaluation—country"). Overall, how do they compare? What is the modal response in each frequency distribution? What substantive conclusions do you reach?

b.   Using the same general technique we employed in the chapter to compare one group with another, compare men's and women's attitudes toward British membership in the European Union (EU).

Exercise 11-8. The chapter on sampling (Chapter 9) discussed the trade-offs involved in selecting a sample size. Roughly speaking the larger the sample, the larger the precision of our estimates of some unknown quantity or confidence in an inference. However, the difficulty and costs of gathering data can increase rapidly as the sample size grows. Consequently, one of the most commonly asked questions is, "How big does my sample have to be?" Estimating the mean provides an example of how the matter can be approached.

Suppose you want to estimate the unknown population mean of a variable Y. Recall that the *standard error of the mean* indicates how much variation there will be in a sample estimate for a given size sample (see Helpful Hint at right). Suppose we want this "error" to be no more than 10 units. (In our notation we want $\hat{\sigma}_{\bar{Y}} = 10$.) Assume, furthermore, that the sample standard deviation (not the standard error!) of the variable we are interested in is $\hat{\sigma}_Y = 20$. How large, under these circumstances, must the sample (N) be in order to meet the requirement that the error be 10 units?

a. Sample for 10: _____

Suppose you wanted to cut the error in half. Now what size N is required? If you wanted to reduce that error by half again (that is, to 2.5), what N is necessary? And again, by half. What is the N? Finally, what about cutting the error all the way to .625 units? Now what sample size do you need?

b. Sample for 5: _____

c. Sample for 2.5: _____

d. Sample for 1.25: _____

e. Sample for .625: _____

Exercise 11-9. Table 11-3 displays some poll results as they were presented in the *Christian Science Monitor*.[3]

What information is missing from this table that might be important in interpreting the results?

_____

_____

_____

_____

_____

_____

_____

_____

_____

TABLE 11-3

Poll Question

How would you grade President Bush's performance in handling the Iraq situation?

	1/04	4/04
Excellent	29%	21%
Good	24	21
Average	16	15
Poor	13	15
Unacceptable	16	28

[3] Liz Marlantes, "Support Eroding for Bush on Iraq," *Christian Science Monitor*, April 9, 2004. Available online at www.csmonitor.com/2004/0409/p01s04-uspo.html. Accessed July 10, 2004.

Exercise 11-10. Define as clearly as possible these statistics. Write a formula if you wish, but try to explain the term in plain language as well.

a. The sample standard deviation.

_____

_____

_____

_____

_____

_____

_____

b. The estimated standard deviation or standard error of the mean.

_____

_____

_____

_____

_____

_____

_____

Exercise 11-11. The last section of Chapter 11 discusses an important problem in social and political research, namely, how to make an inference about a population from the information in a sample. To take one case, suppose your employer, the mayor of a large American city, wants a good estimate of level of satisfaction with public services. This level is measured on a 100-degree "thermometer" with 0 representing total dissatisfaction; 50, neither satisfied nor dissatisfied; and 100, completely satisfied. If the public's average score is below 40, she may abandon her attempt at reelection and retire to private life. You interview a random sample of 100 citizens and find that the mean thermometer level is 45 degrees with a standard deviation of 20 degrees. Should she run again?

a. To help you provide an informed opinion find 95 percent confidence intervals for your estimate. Assume that the scores are normally distributed.[4] (Tip: use the method underlying Table 11-12 in the textbook to construct an interval around the sample mean. As an example, to compute 95 percent intervals, add and subtract 1.96 standard errors from the sample mean.)

_____

_____

_____

_____

_____

b. Now, what do you think? Should the mayor run for reelection? Why?

_____

_____

_____

_____

_____

c. Now suppose that the sample size is 10,000 but the results are the same: the mean is 45 degrees with a standard deviation of 20. Based on this new information would you change your opinion? Why?

_____

_____

_____

_____

_____

---

[4] Strictly speaking, we do not have to assume normality if the sample size is large (say, greater than 75), as it is here.

CHAPTER 12

Measuring Relationships and Testing Hypotheses:
Bivariate Data Analysis

Chapter 12 takes up the investigation of relationships between two variables. Two variables are statistically related if values of the observations for one variable are associated with values of the observations for the other. This chapter gives you a chance to investigate several aspects of two-variable relationships, including strength, direction or shape, and statistical significance.

We mentioned in Chapter 11 that plenty of career opportunities exist for political scientists who have a reasonable understanding of quantitative methods. So if you know a little about crosstabulations, regression analysis, and statistical inference, you may find jobs waiting for you in campaigns, government, consulting firms, industry, and a host of other areas. But experience tells us that in almost every instance employers look for well-trained social scientists who can also clearly, succinctly, and forcefully explain numerical procedures and results to people who do not have much knowledge of (and, frankly, not much interest in) these topics. This ability becomes particularly valuable when someone asks, "Is this an important finding, one I should pay attention to, or can I ignore it?" Hence, we encourage you to think carefully about the answers to the questions posed here and in other chapters.

We offer some advice for translating statistical results into commonsense:

Before responding to the question (or submitting a report to your boss), consider what is being asked. In the real world, people want answers expressed in real-world terms. You have been told that a regression coefficient, for example, can be interpreted as the slope of a line or as indicating how much Y changes for each unit increase or decrease in X. An r measures goodness of fit. But for many people explanations expressed in those terms are gibberish. It is essential, then, that you make sense of statistical terms by placing them in a specific substantive context. Regression and correlation coefficients indicate how and how strongly one thing is related to another. That's their importance. So make sure that you talk about variables, not equations or Greek letters or abstract symbols. Example: write, "income is related to attitudes on taxation," not "X is related to Y."

Go even further to explain the nature of interconnections. Yes, income is correlated with opinions. But how? "Well," you might add, "the wealthier people are, the more they favor cutting taxes, but even the lower and middle classes want some degree of tax relief." This statement is much more informative to a nonstatistician than "There's a positive correlation."

We have suggested numerous times that the definitions of variables determine how we interpret the phenomena under consideration. People want to know if there is a meaningful difference between A and B or they to want to understand how strongly X and Y are connected. Numbers alone won't tell. Only the names and meanings of the variables will. So don't write something like "there is a difference of 10 (or a difference of 10 units)." The difference is of what? Dollars? Years? Pounds? Percents?

In this same vein, variables' measurement scales are critically important. They should be one of the first things you look for and understand. In some cases the meaning of the categories or intervals will be obvious or intuitive, as in "years of formal schooling." In other instances a scale may present some more or less subtle explanatory difficulties. Take income, a variable we discuss several times in the text. In many cases the scale is just "dollars," so "$1,000" has a clear meaning. (But see below.) In other instances a variable may be measured in thousands, millions, or even billions of dollars. (That is, "$10" may stand for 10 million dollars.) It is important that you know exactly which. After all, a change of "10" means one thing when we are talking about simple dollars and quite another when the scale is millions or billions. And complicating matters even further, social scientists often measure variables on abstract or artificial scales. ("Where would you place yourself on this ten-point thermometer of feelings about the president?") If one person's score is 7 and another's 5, they differ. But how important in the world of politics is this difference? As we emphasize below, it is only possible to give a reasoned judgment; there will seldom be a clearly right or wrong answer.

You can help yourself by keeping track of measures of central tendency and variability. If most respondents in a study have values near the mean or median, then one person whose score is two standard deviations away may be unusual and warrant further investigation. Was the individual correctly measured? Is he or she an "extremist?" The two interpretations, which have vastly different substantive implications, can be adjudicated only with thought and perhaps further research.

Don't let one or two measures (e.g., chi-square, r) do all your interpretative work. Instead, try to examine the data as a whole. If you have a contingency table, look for patterns of association within the table's body. Compare different categories of the response patterns. It often happens, for example, that individuals at the "high" and "low" ends of a scale differ greatly in their attitudes. Those in the middle may be more homogeneous. Or it may be the case that response patterns progressively differ as one moves from one end of the table to the other. Whatever the case, this is an important fact that affects the overall interpretation of the data. Similarly, variables having quantitative (ratio and interval) scales should be plotted as they are in Figure 12-3 in the textbook. (Graphing software is so widely available that this shouldn't be a chore.) Among other things you can determine the form of relationships and locate "outlying" observations.

As we noted, assessing "importance" is one of the hardest tasks facing data analysts. There are both statistical and substantive aspects to the problem. And both have to be considered simultaneously. Terms such as "statistical significance" and "explained variation" pertain to observed data, not to people's actual feelings and behavior. Therefore, finding that a chi-square is statistically significant may or may not be important. By the same token the fact that income "explains 60 percent of the variation in political ideology" doesn't necessarily mean we know much about why people are liberals, moderates, and conservatives. Data analysis helps us understand, but it does not replace hard thought about the substance of a topic.

Here are two brief case studies that may tie these ideas together.

1. An investigator wants to know if Americans are more knowledgeable about government and politics than Germans. She conducts a survey of 5,000 citizens in each country (total $N = 10,000$) and discovers that 20 percent of Americans and 25 percent of Germans can name their representative to the local legislature. Statistically speaking, this would be a highly significant difference. But does it have practical importance? Most observers would probably say, "No, there's no functional or meaningful difference. The statistical significance is a product of the huge sample size."

2. A different researcher is studying the impact of political stability on living standards in twenty-five countries in Asia, the Middle East, and Africa. Among other things he has collected data on the number of deaths in 2000 due to domestic political violence and the percentage of the population that has access to clean drinking water. The regression coefficient ($\hat{\beta}$) of "water availability" on deaths from civil disorder is $-.5$. This seems like a small number, and it may even be statistically insignificant. But keep in mind the sign of the coefficient and the measurement scales. For every additional death there is a half percent decline in access to clean drinking water. If there were a causal connection between the two (and we do not assert that there is because this study is totally hypothetical), 10 more deaths in a year would reduce the percentage of the population with healthy water by 5. Think about what would happen if the violence persisted. The lesson is that a "small" numerical value might represent a large effect. It all depends on the substantive context.

Keep these practical tips in mind as you answer the questions in this and the final chapter.

Exercise 12-1. Fill in the blanks.

a. _____ analysis is used to examine the existence of a relationship when both variables are nominal- or ordinal-level measures.

b. In a contingency table, the conventional practice is to make the independent variable the _____ (row/column) variable.

c. If the independent variable is the row variable in a contingency table, the percentages in each _____ (row/column) should add up to 100.

d. Comparison of means and analysis of variance are used to look for a relationship between two variables when the independent variable is a _____ or _____ -level measure and the dependent variable is a _____ or _____ -level measure.

e. _____ analysis is used to see if there is a _____ _____ relationship between two variables if both variables are interval- or ratio-level measures.

Exercise 12-2. Using the hypothetical data given in the table below, create a contingency table in order to examine the relationship between strength of party affiliation and voting in an election. Describe the relationship between voting and strength of party affiliation. Make sure that you include the appropriate percentages as well as the frequencies.

Strength of Party Affiliation (independent variable)	Voting Record (dependent variable)	N
Strong	Voted	95
Strong	did not vote	45
Moderate	voted	72
Moderate	did not vote	88
Weak	voted	53
Weak	did not vote	97

a.   In your opinion is there a relationship? Briefly explain.

_____

_____

_____

_____

_____

Exercise 12-3. Table 12-1 is a contingency table from a computer program that shows the relationship between region and the political party of ninety-nine U.S. senators. (One independent senator is not included.)

TABLE 12-1

Crosstabulation of Senators' Party Identification and Region

Party Identification			Region				
			1 Northeast	2 South	3 Midwest	4 West	Total
PARTYRD	1 Democrat	Count	16	9	14	10	49
		% within region	69.6%	37.5%	53.8%	38.5%	49.5%
	2 Republican	Count	7	15	12	16	50
		% within region	30.4%	62.5%	46.2%	61.5%	50.5%
Total		Count	23	24	26	26	99
		% within region	100.0%	100.0%	100.0%	100.0%	100.0%

Note: Computer-generated table.

a. Do the data indicate that Democratic senators tend to come from different regions from those of Republican senators?

b. If you did not know which region a senator was from, what would be your best guess of his or her party affiliation?

c. Why is lambda an appropriate measure of association to use with the data in the table?

d. Calculate and interpret lambda.

Exercise 12-4. Examine the data presented in Table 12-2.

TABLE 12-2
Crosstabulation of Prayer by Political Ideology

PRAY: How often does R pray	Political Orientation			Total
	1 Liberal	2 Moderate	3 Conservative	
1 Several times a day	33	71	91	195
	18.0%	23.9%	41.7%	27.9%
2 Once a day	53	86	64	203
	29.0%	29.0%	29.4%	29.1%
3 Several times a week	22	48	25	95
	12.0%	16.2%	11.5%	13.6%
4 Once a week	17	18	14	49
	9.3%	6.1%	6.4%	7.0%
5 Less than once a week	55	72	23	150
	30.1%	24.2%	10.6%	21.5%
6 Never	3	2	1	6
	1.6%	.7%	.5%	.9%
Total	183	297	218	698
	100.0%	100.0%	100.0%	100.0%

Note: Computer-generated table.

a. Which is the independent variable? Which is the dependent variable? Describe the relationship between the variables.

_____

_____

_____

_____

_____

_____

_____

_____

_____

_____

b. The gamma value for the data in the table is –.288. What does gamma tell you about the relationship between political orientation and frequency of praying? Why does gamma have a negative sign?

_____

_____

_____

_____

_____

_____

_____

_____

_____

Exercise 12-5.

a. Look at Table 12-3. If there were no relationship between race and opinion about stationing American troops in Iraq, what percentage of whites would you expect to be in favor of keeping troops in Iraq? What percentage of nonwhites? (Refer to pages 362-365 of the main text for more information.)

TABLE 12-3

Relationship between Race and Opinion on Keeping Troops in Iraq

Opinion	Race		Total
	White	Nonwhite	
Keep troops in Iraq	367	56	423
	56.1%	23.5%	47.4%
Bring troops home	287	182	469
	43.9%	76.5%	52.6%
Total	654	238	892
	100%	100%	100%

b. State a null hypothesis for the data in Table 12-3.

c. Calculate the following expected frequencies:

Whites in favor of keeping troops in Iraq: ———————————

Whites in favor of bringing troops home: ———————————

Nonwhites in favor of keeping troops in Iraq: ———————————

Nonwhites in favor of bringing troops home: ———————————

d. Calculate chi-square.

e. Calculate the degrees of freedom for the table.

_____

f. What is the probability of getting a chi-square value of at least the value you have calculated if the null hypothesis were true? What is this probability called? How confi-
dent can you be that the relationship observed in the sample shown in the table also
exists in the population?

_____

_____

_____

_____

_____

g. Briefly explain the statistical and political meaning of these results.

_____

_____

_____

_____

_____

Exercise 12-6. We hear a lot of discussion about "group ratings" of politicians and candidates. The American Civil Liberties Union (ACLU), for example, annually rates members of Congress on their support and opposition to legislation about civil liberties (e.g., freedom of speech). Those senators and representatives who vote against laws and amendments banning flag burning get higher scores than those who do not.

Following the instructions provided to you by your instructor regarding which statistics software package to use, access the CD-ROM and find the file "Senate.dat" and examine the relationship between a senator's party affiliation and score on the ACLU scorecard. Use the variable "PARTYRD," which excludes independents from the analysis, as the measure of senators' party affiliation.

a.   What level of measurement is PARTYRD?

_____

b.   What is the level of measurement for ACLU?

_____

c.   Write a hypothesis about the relationship between party and ACLU scorecard scores.

_____

d.   What statistical procedures would you use to see if there is a relationship between the variables and how strong a relationship it is?

_____

_____

_____

_____

_____

e.   It is *not* appropriate to use a test of statistical significance for the data. Why not?

_____

_____

f.   Run the appropriate statistical analyses and then discuss your results in substantive terms.

Exercise 12-7. Using the same data set as in exercise 12-6, let's examine the relationship between senators' scores on the ACLU and American Conservative Union (ACU) score-cards. (Whereas the ACLU is a liberal/liberties group on civil liberties issues, the ACU is a politically conservative organization.)

a.   Write a hypothesis about the association between senators' ACLU and ACU scores. Remember, be as specific as possible about how the variables are associated.

_____

_____

b.   What level of measurement is each of the variables?

_____

_____

c. What type of analysis is appropriate for examining the relationship between the variables?

_____

_____

d. What measure(s) of association is (are) appropriate to use? Will the measure(s) have a sign? Using the data and appropriate software find this (these) measure(s) and report it (them) here.

_____

_____

e. Run the analysis using ACLU scores as the *dependent* variable, and discuss your results. For every 1 percent change in the ACU score how much change is there in the ACLU score? When the ACU score is 0, what is the predicted ACLU score? If a senator has a score of 10 on the ACU rating, what would you predict his or her score to be on the ACLU scale?

_____

f. Your instructor may suggest that you create a scatterplot showing the data. You may be able to draw the regression line over the data points. (Check the software.) This will give you an idea of how well the line fits the data.

g. Interpret the results.

Exercise 12-8. Referring to the research of several political scientists, David Brooks, a *New York Times* columnist, writes, "Party affiliation even shapes people's perceptions of reality . . . people's perceptions are blatantly biased by partisanship."[1] The 2000 American National Election Study located on the CD-ROM provides data to verify this assertion. To do this assignment you will of course need software that can crosstabulate two variables and calculate elementary statistics. Consult your instructor or laboratory assistant for help. If you refer to the guide to this data set ("anes2000readme.txt") you will find that "Party Identification" (variable 24) measures both the strength and direction of political party affiliation. Other variables represent measures of perceptions. Try to see if Brooks's statement holds water.

a. At the time of the 2000 presidential election a Democrat, Bill Clinton, occupied the White House. Voters rightly or wrongly connect the past performance of the economy to the presidency. So use the variable "Economy During Past Year" (variable 19) to form a contingency or crosstabulation table of party identification and perceptions of economic performance. Print or place a properly labeled and formatted

[1] David Brooks, "Circling the Wagons," *New York Times*, June 5, 2004, 25.

table in the space below. (Tip: You don't have to enter the raw frequencies in each cell, just the appropriate percentages. But you should include the marginal frequencies for the independent variable.)

b. What is the chi-square for this table?

Chi-square = ———————————— with ————————————
degrees of freedom. What does the chi-square mean in *both* statistical *and* substantive terms?

———

———

———

———

c.   What is gamma? ————————————————. What is Kendall's tau-b?
     ————————————————. What do these measures tell you?

     ——

     ——

d.   Now use the variable "Gore: Leader?" (variable 27) to test the hypothesis about par-
     tisanship's effects on perceptions. In the space below print or carefully place a table
     that shows the relationship between party identification and beliefs about Al Gore
     being a "strong leader."

e. What is the chi-square for this table? Chi-square = _____
    with _____ degrees of freedom. What does the chi-square
    mean in statistical terms? What is the practical or theoretical import of the findings?
    As an example, what do the results imply about the effectiveness of television com-
    mercials that attack a candidate's leadership abilities? Are they likely to "work" on all
    voters equally? Under what conditions?

    _____

    _____

    _____

    _____

    _____

f. What is gamma? _____. What is Kendall's tau-b?
    _____. What do these measures tell you?

    _____

    _____

    _____

    _____

    _____

Exercise 12-9. It might be instructive to explore the issue in Exercise 12-7 in a comparative context. The data from the "British Election Study 2001" offer a chance to do so. These data are available on the CD-ROM in a couple of formats: "bes2001.dat" and "bes2001.por," an SPSS file. A text file, "bescodebook.txt" describes the variables. (Chapter 9 of this workbook describes these files in more detail.)

At the time of the 2001 general elections, Tony Blair's Labour Party controlled Parliament and hence the government. There are two other major parties in Britain, the Conservative and the Liberal Democrat. Try to determine if party identification (variable 1) is related to variable 6, "How do you think the general economic situation in this country has changed over the last 12 months?"

(Tip: As in the United States there are several "minor" or "lesser" parties in Britain. But to simplify your analysis we suggest you eliminate all the party identifiers other than Labour, Conservative, and Liberal Democrat.)

a.   In the space below print or place the contingency or crosstabulation table.

b. What is your interpretation? Do the data support the assertion that party identification colors perceptions of political and economic affairs?

_____

_____

_____

_____

_____

c. What are the chi-square and degrees of freedom for this table? What do they mean in statistical and substantive terms?

_____

_____

_____

_____

_____

d. Obtain or calculate lambda and interpret (both statistically and substantively) its meaning in this context.

_____

_____

_____

_____

_____

Exercise 12-10. One of the problems with just throwing data in a computer, pressing a button, and then waiting "to see what happens" is that relationships or correlations occasionally turn up without apparent rhyme or reason. We've mentioned a couple of times that if you correlated birth rates and stork populations in geographical regions of some countries you might find a relationship. We called that result "spurious" to indicate there was no cause-and-effect connection between the two variables. But the term "spurious," or false, may be too strong to apply to an association that is empirically observed. After all, it *is* real; we do see it. So what is necessary is to interpret the observed relation; to explain *why* the variables are related.

This assignment gives you a chance to look at a statistical relationship that at first sight may not make a good deal of substantive sense. It requires you to think about the meaning of variables and why they might be related. It also offers a chance to calculate some common statistics used in regression analysis.

Table 12-4 presents data from twenty-three Maryland counties. (We saw the full table in this workbook's Chapter 11, Table 11-2.) This time let's see if there is a relationship between water consumption (in gallons per day per person) and the crime rate, two variables that one would expect would have no connection. Besides the data, the table contains space for calculations if your instructor wants you to do them by hand. Otherwise, you can load the data ("marylandcounty.dat") and analyze "serious crimes known to the police" (variable 2 in the file) and "consumptive water use in millions of gallons per day" (variable 6). (The first row of this file contains variable

TABLE 12-4
Crime Rates and Water Use in Twenty-three Maryland Counties

County	Crime Rate[a] (X)	X²	Water Use[b] (Y)	Y²	XY
Allegany	3311	___	8	___	___
Anne Arundel	4457	___	7	___	___
Baltimore	4982	___	42	___	___
Calvert	2315	___	17	___	___
Caroline	3845	___	17	___	___
Carroll	2237	___	3	___	___
Cecil	3569	___	2	___	___
Charles	3699	___	12	___	___
Dorchester	3931	___	14	___	___
Frederick	2531	___	5	___	___
Garrett	1756	___	1	___	___
Harford	2516	___	3	___	___
Howard	3264	___	3	___	___
Kent	1931	___	4	___	___
Montgomery	3217	___	14	___	___
Prince Georges	6257	___	27	___	___
Queen Annes	3056	___	10	___	___
St. Marys	2387	___	1	___	___
Somerset	3400	___	3	___	___
Talbot	3438	___	2	___	___
Washington	2571	___	4	___	___
Wicomico	5278	___	9	___	___
Worcester	6168	___	4	___	___

Source: Bureau of the Census, *City and County Data Book, 2000.* Available online at www.census.gov/statab/www/ ccdb.html. Accessed July 10, 2004.

[a] Serious crime rate per 100,000 resident population, 1999.
[b] Consumptive water use, millions of gallons per day.

names. Although some statistical programs are lenient, you might have to use an editor to remove the names before loading the data. In addition, there is a portable SPSS file of the same data, "marylandcounty.por.") In this exercise interest lies in the pattern of association between crime rates and water use, not cause and effect. Therefore, let's treat crime as the independent variable and water use as the dependent variable. This designation is admittedly arbitrary, but in order for everyone to be on the same page, so to speak, make sure that you treat your variables this way: crime is X and water use is Y.

a. On a piece of graph paper plot the two variables. Or, if your instructor wishes or permits, have your software prepare a scatter plot of X versus Y. (It might be instructive to compare your hand-drawn plot with the computer-generated one.) For both cases, keep in mind what we said about the placement of the dependent and independent variables. Look at Figures 12-3, 12-10, and 12-12 in the textbook for guidance. Also recall what was said in Chapter 11 about clearly and fully labeling axes and keeping embellishments to a minimum. Attach the plot to your assignment according to your instructor's requirements.

b. Examine the plot. What type of relationship (if any) do you see? That is, is it linear, positive, etc.? Consult the discussion of Figure 12-11 in the textbook for help.

    _____

    _____

c. Imagine a regression line passing through the "middle" of the points. Would the

    slope be positive or negative? _____

d. Using either hand calculations or a computer, find the following quantities:

    Sum of X (ΣX): _____

    Sum of X squared (ΣX^2): _____

    Sum of Y (ΣY): _____

    Sum of Y squared (ΣY^2): _____

    Sum of X times Y (ΣXY) : _____

    N: _____

e.   What is the estimated regression coefficient (slope)? _____

f.   Give a statistical and substantive interpretation of this number:

_____

_____

_____

_____

g.   What is the estimated regression constant (intercept) for these data? Does it make sense in real-world terms?

_____

_____

_____

_____

h.   What is R-squared for this relationship? _____

i.   Supply a statistical and substantive interpretation of this measure.

_____

_____

_____

_____

j. If you found a relationship between these two variables, what might explain it? Surely, crimes don't *cause* people to consume more or less water. Can you think of an explanation? (Tip: There are two ideas to consider. First, where is water most likely to be consumed? And what's apt to characterize living conditions in those same places? Second, look carefully at the plot. Do you see one or more observations that perhaps do not fit the overall pattern?)

_____

_____

_____

_____

_____

_____

_____

_____

_____

_____

_____

_____

k. For a moment assume that the twenty-three counties are a random sample drawn from some universe or population of counties. Suppose we told you that the standard error of the regression coefficient was .0015 and that the corresponding observed t was 2.63 with 21 degrees of freedom. Would these results be grounds for rejecting the null hypothesis that the population regression coefficient ($\beta_{water.crime}$) is zero? Why?

_____

_____

_____

_____

_____

_____

_____

Exercise 12-11. Do political party leaders represent their rank-and-file members? Do their opinions and stands on issues generally agree with their supporters? Or are they more liberal or conservative? Richard Herrera investigated this question by comparing the mean views of delegates to the 1988 Democratic Party convention, presumably a good cross-section of party leaders, with those of Democratic voters.[2] He hypothesized that if leaders are out of touch with followers, there will be a difference between their average issue positions. A small portion of his results can be seen in Table 12-5.

TABLE 12-5

Mean Views of Democratic Delegates and Democratic Voters, 1988

Issue	Mean Delegate View	Mean Partisan Voter View	Mean Difference and Significance
Defense spending	2.33	3.11	−.78**
Get along with Russia	2.24	3.23	−.99**
Government helps blacks	2.86	1.92	−.94**
Place of women	1.47	2.46	−.99**

Source: Richard Herrera, "Are 'Superdelegates' Super?" _Political Behavior_ 16 (March 1994): 88.

** = Significant at .01 level.

---

[2] Richard Herrera, "Are 'Superdelegates' Super?" _Political Behavior_ 16 (March 1994): 79–92.

The mean delegate and partisan voter responses are given on 7-point scales. For instance, both delegates and a random sample of Democratic voters were asked about their opinions on defense spending. A "1" on the scale represents the most "liberal" position (i.e., cut defense spending), whereas "7" is the most "conservative" stance. If everyone in a particular group was liberal, the mean score would be 1. The other questions, for which respondents could reply on similar 7-point scales, were: "Should we try to get along with Russia" (1), or is this a "big mistake" (7); "Should the government in Washington make every effort to improve the social and economic position of blacks" (1), or should there be "no special effort" (7); and "Should women have an equal role with men in running business, industry, or government" (1), or is women's "place in the home" (7). The last column represents the difference in means between delegates and voters. The author writes that the symbol ** means "difference is significant at $p < .01$." [3] Try to make sense of these results.

a. What general hypothesis is the author investigating?

_____

_____

_____

b. What statistical hypothesis does each line of the table test?

_____

c. Which of these statistical hypotheses should Herrera reject and why?

_____

_____

_____

---

[3] Although it may be losing favor, the use of stars or other typographical symbols has, in the past, been a common way to report significance. An asterisk (*), for instance, conveys the idea that the *statistical* hypothesis (e.g., statistical independence) has been rejected at the .05 level. But it is far preferable for you to indicate the attained or observed probability of the sample result if the null hypothesis is true. It's analogous to a friend who tells you that the Baltimore Orioles beat the New York Yankees. That may be good or bad news, but the next question is, "Okay, what was the final *score*?" So rather than reporting that a result is significant at the .05 level, indicate as closely as you can the actual probability under the null hypothesis. It might be, say, .04, which is barely significant at the .05 level, or it might be .002, which is highly significant at that level. Most software reports the attained probability, so why not include it in your report?

d. So far you have considered statistical hypotheses: should they be rejected or not? Now translate these results into terms an average citizen can understand. What, in short, do the results say about Democratic leaders and average party voters? (Tip: Always keep in mind the meaning of the questions and the scales. In other words, if one person has a higher score on, say, the defense spending issue than another individual, would you say the first was more "liberal" or "conservative" than the second?)

_____

_____

_____

_____

_____

Searching for Complete Explanations and Causal Knowledge:

Multivariate Analysis

In Chapter 13 we presented several different statistical methods or "models" for investigating relationships involving a dependent variable and more than a single independent variable. Multivariate analysis helps researchers to discover spurious relationships, to measure the effect of changes in multiple independent variables on a dependent variable, and, generally, to strengthen claims about causal relationships. Multivariate statistical procedures allow researchers to control statistically for other factors instead of controlling other factors experimentally. Substitution of statistical control for experimental control is not a perfect solution in the quest to establish causal explanations for political phenomena and, therefore, results and claims based on statistical evidence must be scrutinized carefully.

As with bivariate data analysis, the choice of analytical procedure depends on the way variables, particularly the dependent variable, are measured:

■ Contingency table analysis is used when the data are categorical, that is, the variables have categories. This method quickly becomes unwieldy and difficult to interpret as the number of tables and cells increases and the number of cases or observations in cells decreases.

■ Two-way analysis of variance is used to assess the extent to which two or more categorical independent variables explain the variance in a numerical dependent variable.

■ Linear multiple regression investigates whether there is a linear relationship between a numerically measured dependent variable and multiple independent variables and allows researchers to assess how much a one-unit change in an independent variable changes the dependent variable when all the other variables have been taken into account or controlled. So-called dummy variables are used when there are categorical independent variables.

■ A logistic regression model is used when the dependent variable is a dichotomy (or binary variable with values of 0 or 1) and estimates the probability that the dependent variable equals 1 as a linear function of the independent variables.

Also, as with bivariate data analysis, we are interested in the strength of the relationship, or how well the model "fits" the data, and in the statistical significance of our findings.

While some models and statistical procedures can get quite complicated, with some practice you will be able to use at least the simpler ones and to interpret their results. The following exercises will give you practice in deciding which procedure is appropriate to use, how to relate your data to the procedure, and how to interpret the results of the analyses.

Exercise 13-1. Here are a few research hypotheses and designs. For each one, explain what would be an appropriate statistical analytic tool and why. (Tip: What are the dependent and independent variables and how are they measured?)

a. An investigator believes guerrilla wars or insurgencies are caused mainly by rather sudden decreases in the economic standard of living of large numbers of society members.[1] Data collected from fifty-five nations consist of the outbreak or occurrence of domestic violence in a given year (yes or no) and measures of changes in income, poverty, employment, and manufacturing and agricultural output for the previous year.

_____

_____

_____

_____

_____

[1] Incidentally, for a classic statement of this hypothesis see Crane Brinton, *The Anatomy of Revolution*, rev. and expanded ed. (Englewood Cliffs, N.J.: Prentice Hall, 1965).

b. A social scientist wonders if the Sun Belt states are as politically conservative today as they are reputed to be. She believes that apart from perhaps social issues the opinions and beliefs of people in different regions are roughly the same. Moreover, she thinks that any variation among regions stems mainly from differences in the social class composition of the citizens living in those places. Her data are in the "American National Election Study 2000" data file that has categorical measures of region, attitudes on economic issues, and demographic characteristics such as income, education, and ethnicity.[2] What would be a good way to explore this hypothesis with these data?

_____

_____

_____

_____

_____

c. A Washington policy organization ("think tank") wants to know why some states have more generous health care benefits for the poor than others. It hypothesizes that two general factors explain the difference, states' overall political philosophy (degree of liberalism, for example) and economic capacity. The more liberal and wealthy a state, the more generous its health programs. The group's research firm has numerical indicators of health spending per capita for the poor, ideology,[3] percentage voting Democratic in national and state elections for the last ten years, per capita income, and economic growth over the last year. What method do you suggest?

_____

_____

_____

_____

_____

---

[2] An aside: this topic would make a great research project for a student with access to the American National Election data and statistical software.

[3] Measures of states' ideology actually exist and are widely used. See, for example, Gerald C. Wright, Robert S. Erikson, and John P. McIver, "Measuring State Partisanship and Ideology with Survey Data," *Journal of Politics* 47 (1985): 469–489. Also see William D. Berry, Evan J. Rinquist, Richard C. Fording, and Russell L. Hanson, "Measuring Citizen and Government Ideology in the American States, 1960–93," *American Journal of Political Science* 42 (1998): 327–348.

PREPARING AND ORGANIZING A MULTIVARIATE ANALYSIS

Analyzing more than two variables at a time can be a daunting chore, even for experienced data analysts. The secret, we believe, is the same as for any academic undertaking: think before acting. In the case of multivariate analysis, careful planning is of utmost importance. Hence, we offer a few suggestions to help you organize your research:

- As we discussed in previous chapters of *Political Science Research Methods,* it is essential that you state a few working hypotheses. If you sit in front of a computer before organizing your thoughts, you will soon be drowned in printout. We guarantee it.
- If you are given a data set, pick a likely dependent variable—something that might be important to understand or explain. Then ask yourself which of the other variables in the file might be related to it. If you are starting from scratch, you have more leeway. But in any case, try to convert these ideas into substantive hypotheses. (Remember, a hypothesis is a tentative statement subject to verification. The result of the test is actually less important than starting with a meaningful proposition. Why? Because whether one accepts or rejects it, something of value has still been learned. Testing trivial propositions [e.g., poverty among children is correlated with poverty among families] doesn't advance our knowledge of anything.)
- Similarly, think carefully about what would be appropriate indicators of general explanatory factors. Suppose, for instance, you believe that high crime rates encourage people to leave cities for the suburbs or countryside. Then if you are trying to explain migration to the suburbs, one of your independent variables would be crime, which can be measured by, say, homicide rates or property lost to theft. Whatever the case, think of broad explanatory factors and empirical indicators of them.
- Sometimes the choice of variables is straightforward. Frequently, however, you may need your imagination to construct indicators. Suppose you theorize that *changes* in population density explain something but that data at your disposal only contain the actual populations and areas of cities for 1994 and 2004. You first need to compute a density for each year by dividing total population by area to obtain, say, persons per square mile. Then you could calculate another indicator, "percent change in population density from 1994 to 2004."[4] Most software makes these sorts of transformations easy.
- Remember that the data are empirical *indicators* of underlying theoretical concepts. You can't expect them to be perfectly or even strongly related to the dependent variable or to one another. In general, if you find a model that explains 40 to 50 percent of the statistical variation in Y, you will be doing well.

d. A student in a political communications class wants to know if a newspaper's size, as measured by average weekly circulation, affected its coverage of the 2004 National Democratic Convention, as indicated by the average number of column inches it devotes to the subject in the month of July. He has spent considerable time collecting these data for forty papers throughout the United States. But he wonders if coverage will also be influenced by the papers' political partisanship and region, for which he has only indicator or categorical variables. (Party bias, for instance, is coded into three categories—"pro-Democratic," "neutral," and "pro-Republican"—whereas region is indexed simply as 0 for "Non-South" and 1 for "South.") Can you help this person pick an appropriate statistical strategy for investigating the hypothesis? How would your strategy handle the independent variables?

---

[4] We recommend the "log percent change," which is $\log_{10}$ (first number/second number) X 100, where $\log_{10}$ is the logarithm to the base 10.

- We strongly urge you to analyze each variable individually, especially the dependent variable. Use the methods described in Chapter 11 of the textbook.
- If your analysis involves multiple regression, first obtain plots of all the variables against each other. Doing so will reveal important aspects of the relationships, such as curvilinearity, the existence of outlying points, and the lack of variation in one or both variables. All these aspects can and should be taken into consideration. See the previous exercises for examples of what to expect. Some software allows you to identify interactively by placing the cursor over a point on the graph and clicking. (Your instructor or lab assistant will help.)
- It is permissible, even advisable in some instances, to delete the outlying cases if you can do so on substantive grounds. Or, you can sometimes transform variables. Have you noticed, for instance, that some authors we cite in this book analyze not income but the *logarithm* of income. Doing so can mitigate the effects of a few very large numbers on a statistical procedure. One of the unfortunate properties of regression as we have introduced it is that it can be very sensitive to extreme scores. Hence, you may find that a statistical result changes considerably after adjusting the data.[5] *Just be sure to describe your methods fully in your report.*
- It helps to obtain a correlation matrix of your variables. This table will point to variables that are not related to much of anything and that might be dropped from the analysis. Equally important, correlation coefficients will help you decide whether an independent variable is related *in the way* your hypothesis predicts. If there should be a negative relationship, for instance, and the correlation is positive, your starting assumption may be wrong or you may have to look more carefully at the variable's definition.
- A correlation and a plot can also flag another possible problem. Sometimes two independent variables are so highly correlated that they are practically equivalent to each other, and including both in a regression model just adds redundancy; no separate information gets included. After all, if you regress height on weight measured in pounds *and* in kilograms, you just have two versions of one concept. Thus, if you spot high intercorrelations among the independent variables, ask if they are measuring the same thing or represent interesting substantive relationships.

Your final model may be much simpler than your initial expectations. That's probably a good thing because the goal of science is to find the simplest equation that has the highest predictive capacity. It is not important to include lots and lots of variables. One technique is to add or subtract one variable at a time and determine if it appreciably changes the model.[6] You may be able to eliminate quite a few variables this way, thereby reducing complexity.

---

[5] Trust us: far from "cooking the books" this maneuver is acceptable statistical practice in many instances.
[6] Lots of software have procedures for automating this process, but we don't recommend using them at this stage.

Exercise 13-2. Carefully consider the following situations and answer the questions.

a. A researcher suspects that the positive correlation between a numerical scale of racial intolerance and number of hours per week of television viewing is spurious due to education. He thus controls for the number of years of formal schooling. If his supposition about spuriousness is correct, the partial regression coefficient between tolerance and viewing hours controlling for education will have about what numerical value and sign?

_____

b. The regression coefficients of turnout in Senate elections in 1992 on various variables are presented in Table 13-8 of the textbook. In which of the following states would turnout be predicted to be highest? Why? (Tip: Use the least squares equation to predict turnout.)

STATE 1: Campaign tone = –1; turnout = 50 percent; mail-back rate = 75 percent; region = South; college education = 60 percent; logarithm incumbent's spending = .5; closeness of election = .04.

STATE 2: Campaign tone = 1; turnout = 55 percent; mail-back rate = 85 percent; region = non-South; college education = 75 percent; logarithm incumbent's spending = .57; closeness of election = .0004.

(Tip: Just follow the chapter's examples of finding predicted values.)

_____

c. You and your best friend are working on a joint project about the role of religion in American politics. In particular, you want to know if people of different religious faiths disagree with respect to their evaluations of various political leaders and groups. You suggest using the 2002 American National Election Study because it has feeling thermometers for many public officials, interest groups, and parties. These variables can be treated as numeric, since the respondents can place themselves anywhere on a 100-degree (point) scale. (Look at the "anes2000" files on the CD-ROM for examples.) But your friend objects that the main independent variable is nominal, and respondents are simply assigned to the categories "Protestant," "Catholic," "Jewish," "None," and "Other."[7] He's worried that you won't be able to take advantage of regression analysis, which the instructor wants you to use. Do you have an answer for this person's concern? What is it? How can you regress, say, feelings toward George Bush on religion? Be specific to demonstrate your knowledge of the method.

_____

_____

_____

_____

_____

[7] The study actually has many codes for religion, but assume you want to use just those five.

Exercise 13-3. Your boss has asked you to critique a paper, "The Causes of Crime in Urban America." The authors have data on about seventy-five cities. Among many other analyses, there is a regression of Y, "violent crime rate (offenses per 100 thousand population in 1992)" on X_1, "per capita income in central cities" and X_2, "per capita expenditures for public safety." (These data, by the way, can be found on the CD-ROM under the name "stateofcities.dat" or "stateofcities.por.")[8] Luckily some summary statistics for the variables have been supplied in an appendix to the report:

a. The paper reports that the partial regression coefficient of crime on per capita income is –.0076. Does this number mean that economic well-being in a city is unrelated to crime? Explain.

_____

_____

_____

_____

_____

b. The standard error of this partial regression coefficient is .041. What is the observed t?

_____

_____

Variable	Valid Cases	Minimum	Maximum	Mean	Standard Deviation
Per capita safety expenditures (Y)	77	$101	$1,133	$280.43	$128.018
Per capita income (X_1)	77	$9,258	$19,695	$13,679.56	$2,410.431
Crime rate (X_2)	69	141	3859	1,573.00	88.158

Source: Norman Glickman, Michael Lahr, and Elvin Wyly, "The State of the Nation's Cities: Database and Machine Readable Documentation," Version 2a (January 1998), Center for Urban Policy Research, Rutgers University. Available online at http://policy.rutgers.edu/cupr/sonc/sonc.htm.

[8] The data are from Norman J. Glickman, Michael Lahr, and Elvin Wyly, "The State of the Nation's Cities: Database and Machine Readable Documentation," Version 2a (January 1998), Center for Urban Policy Research, Rutgers University. Available online at http://policy.rutgers.edu/cupr/sonc/sonc.htm.

c. Assuming that there is a constant and two independent variables in the equation and $N = 66$ for this particular model, would you reject the null hypothesis that the population partial regression coefficient is 0 based on a two-tailed test at the .05 level? Why?

---

d. There is an additional variable in the model, per capita city government spending on public safety (e.g., police and fire protection). The partial regression coefficient of crime on this variable is 3.090. What does this result mean in substantive terms? More specifically, does it represent evidence of a cause-and-effect relationship? Why?

---

e. The standard error of the partial regression coefficient of Y on X_2 is .749. Knowing this do you think the null hypothesis of no partial linear association between crime and public safety spending should be rejected? Why?

f. You notice that the report concludes that expenditures for police have a greater impact on crime than a city's standard of living. To make the point, the authors mention that the expenditure standardized regression coefficient is twice the size of the one for per capita income, but, strangely, they do not report the actual values. Can you calculate them? And more important, is there any reason at all to make that inference based on these data? (Tip: Look at the table for the statistics you need. Note, however, that that table contains some extra information. You need to select the right statistics. Refer to the section on standardization.)

_____

_____

_____

_____

_____

Exercise 13-4. Below are some "working" plots that show the relationship between two variables. (By "working" we mean graphs that are used in the preliminary steps of an analysis, not presentation graphics.) The data pertain to 435 congressional districts in the United States.[9] For each plot answer the questions that follow.

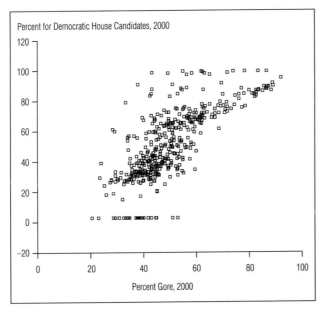

[9] The data are from Kenneth Janda, "Voting in 2000 by Congressional District." Available online at www.janda. org/c10/data%20sets/Congress/cd2000.html. Accessed July 31, 2004.

a. What are the nature and direction of the relationship? _____

    What would be the sign of the regression coefficient applied to these data? _____

b. Give a brief interpretation of the relationship.

    _____

    _____

    _____

c. Look carefully at the graph. Do you see anything that might affect the analysis and interpretation of the data?

    _____

    _____

    _____

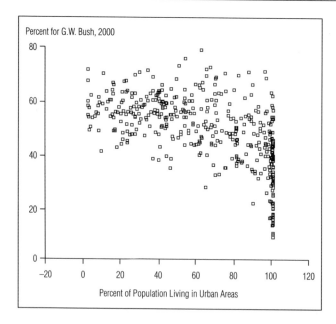

d. What is the direction of the relationship or correlation? _____

    If you performed a regression analysis on these data, what would be the sign of the regression coefficient or slope? _____

e. Briefly describe the relationship in commonsense terms.

_____

_____

_____

f. Carefully examine the plot. Can you find an aspect of the data that might be obscuring the relationship? What is it?

_____

_____

_____

g. Can you think of another, third variable or factor that might "explain" or account for this relationship? What is it? Explain. (Tip: Think about spurious correlation.)

_____

_____

_____

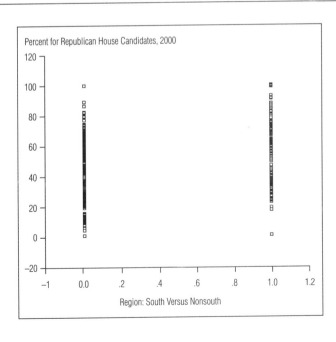

h. In the graph on page 155, what's going on in the plot of region (0 = non-South, 1 = South) and percentages for Republican candidates? Is it "valid"? Is it helpful? Briefly explain. How would you analyze these data, if indeed they could be analyzed, using the techniques discussed in Chapters 12 and 13 of the textbook?

_____

_____

_____

_____

_____

_____

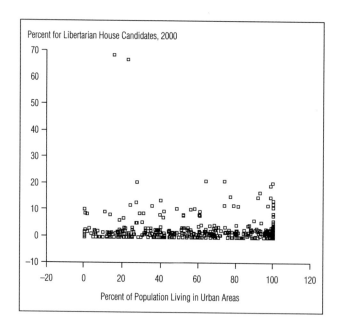

Percent for Libertarian House Candidates, 2000

(x-axis) Percent of Population Living in Urban Areas

i. What do you make of this graph? About what, do you suppose, the correlation coefficient between the variables would be? Provide a brief substantive interpretation.

_____

_____

_____

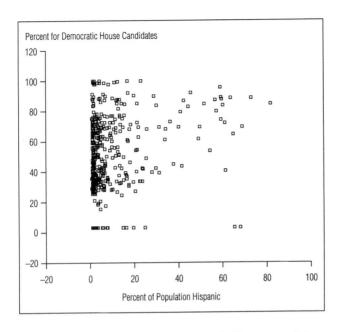

j. Finally, consider the graph concerning Democratic House candidates and Hispanics. Can you discern a relationship? What feature of the independent variable stands out most? About what values would the correlation and regression coefficients between the variables have?

_____

_____

_____

_____

_____

Exercise 13-5. Martin Gilens and Craig Hertzman raise a crucial point for judging the condition of American democracy. They studied news coverage of the 1996 Telecommunications Act, which among other things loosened restrictions on the number of television stations a media corporation could own. Some companies own both newspapers and local TV stations, whereas others do not. The passage of the law, the authors assert, meant that "on average the loosening of ownership caps in the 1996 Telecom Bill benefited media companies that already owned many television stations, and did not benefit (and may have hurt) companies that did not own TV stations." [10]

Some of their findings "strongly indicate a relationship between the financial interests of newspaper owners and the content of their papers' news coverage." This is not a matter of editorial content. Instead, the study's authors believe that what appears and *does not* appear in a paper's news sections may reflect the economic self-interests of the publisher and not inherent newsworthiness or the needs of the public. But they are aware that the connection between financial interest and news content may be "spurious, due to other characteristics of the newspapers." [11]

To check this possibility they conducted a multivariate analysis, a portion of which appears in the table below. The unit of analysis (27 in all) is "newspaper." The dependent variable is the proportion of a paper's coverage of the act that was "negative" (that is, discussed the possible adverse consequences of the act). One of the independent variables was total weekly circulation, which provides an indicator of a paper's revenues, which in turn determine the size of its "news hole" or space for news content. ("Papers with higher circulations and larger news holes might be expected to publish more information about the telecommunications legislation and might mention a higher percentage of negative consequences as a result.") [12] They also looked at presidential candidate endorsements as a proxy measure of the paper's political leanings, and the percentage of revenue from broadcast television "to test the possibility that reporting on [the bill] was influenced less by the number of stations owned than by the parent company's economic dependence on TV revenue." [13] The investigators broke the "main" explanatory factor, ownership of television stations, into two dummy variables:

Substantial =   1 if company has 9 or more TV stations in 1995;
                  0 if company owned none.
Limited =   1 if company owned 2 to 5 TV stations in 1995;
                  0 if company owned none. [14]

---

[10] Martin Gilens and Craig Hertzman, "Corporate Ownership and News Bias: Newspaper Coverage of the 1996 Telecommunications Act," *Journal of Politics* 62 (May 2000): 372.
[11] Ibid.
[12] Ibid.
[13] Ibid.
[14] It is not really clear why Gilens and Hertzman chose this particular way to "measure" ownership, but the interpretation of the results is straightforward if one keeps in mind the definition of dummy variables. Gilens and Hertzman, "Corporate Ownership and News Bias," table 3, p. 382.

Assume that they have a random sample of newspapers. Here is part of the results from their regression analysis plus space to write some of your answers.

	Estimated Coefficient	Standard Error	t Statistic	Level of Significance (two-tailed)[a]
Substantial	−.39	.13		
Limited	−.23	.12		
Circulation	.04	.02		
Endorsement	.04	.05		
Percent of revenue from TV	−.05	.35		
$R^2 = .35$; $N = 27$.				

[a]The researchers used a one-tailed test.

a. Write a model or equation for the predicted value of the proportion of negative coverage. (They didn't report a constant so just ignore that coefficient.)

_____

_____

_____

_____

_____

_____

b. Interpret the R^2:

_____

_____

_____

_____

_____

_____

c. Interpret in statistical and substantive terms the coefficients for substantial and limited ownership. (Tip: Refer to the discussion of dummy variables in Chapter 13 of the textbook. Try to understand them using the logic employed in that section.)

_____

_____

_____

_____

_____

_____

d. What are the observed *t* values? Print them in the table above.

e. If you wanted to test each coefficient for significance, using a two-tailed test, what would be the critical *t* at the .05 level? (It's hard to tell from the authors' explanation, so assume 22 degrees of freedom.) _____

Which of the coefficients is significant at that level? Indicate with a "Yes." Better still, give the level of significance.

_____

_____

Exercise 13-6. A speaker at a lecture declares that no statistical evidence whatever demonstrates that the death penalty discriminates against minorities. When pressed on the point she shows a slide with the following table.[15] The subjects were 326 defendants indicted for murder in Florida during 1976 and 1977.

	Defendant's Race	
Death penalty?	White	Black
Yes	19	17
No	141	149

a. Do these data show a relationship between race and receiving the death penalty? Explain verbally and with a table and an appropriate test statistic.

_____

_____

_____

_____

_____

_____

_____

_____

[15] Actually, these are "real" data first presented by M. Radlet, "Racial Characteristics and the Imposition of the Death Penalty," *American Sociological Review* 46 (1981): 918–927, cited in Alan Agresti, *Analysis of Ordinal Categorical Data* (New York: Wiley, 1984): 6.

Now suppose another panelist exclaims, "Wait a minute! These data only tell part of the story. If they are broken down by the race of the *victim* as well, we see that there is discrimination." He presents the following data:[16]

Death Penalty? (Y)	Victim's Race (Z)			
	White Defendant's race (X)		Black Defendant's race (X)	
	White	Black	White	Black
Yes	19	11	0	6
No	132	52	9	97
Total	151	63	9	103

b. Can you interpret this table? What, if anything, does it say about the discriminatory effects of the application of the death penalty in Florida during that time. (Tip: Look at each subtable one at a time and calculate percentages.)

_____

_____

_____

_____

_____

_____

_____

_____

[16] Agresti, *Analysis of Ordinal Categorical Data,* 32.

Exercise 13-7. Suppose that for a comparative government class you want to study globalization's impact on citizens' political beliefs and behavior. You decide to concentrate on Britain's membership in the European Union, a transnational organization of European states that some Britons fear will infringe on British sovereignty. In particular, you want to know if positions on this issue affected party and candidate choices in the 2001 British general election. The table below *summarizes* the results of a crosstabulation of responses to the question "Overall, do you approve or disapprove of Britain's membership in the European Union?" and the party the respondents voted for in that election (Labour, Liberal Democrat, and Conservative). Your hypothesis is that those who support membership in the EU will vote Labour, whereas those against it will support the conservatives. (These numbers come from the "British Election Study 2001" that is on the CD-ROM under the name "bes2001.dat" or "bes2001.por." We used this file in previous chapters of this workbook.)

Chi-square	df	Tau-b	Gamma	N
160.516	8	.190	.274	1,918

a. Try to replicate our findings in the table above. *Note:* we *eliminated* all the minor parties (i.e., Greens, SNP, Plaid Cymru, and "other") as well as "none." Your tables won't match ours exactly unless you do the same.[17] Why?

b. More important, interpret the results in the table. Supply both a statistical *and* a substantive answer to the question "Is there a relationship between opinions on the EU and the direction of the vote?"

_____

_____

_____

_____

_____

---

[17] We coded the vote variable this way: 1 = "Labour," 2 = "Liberal Democrat," and 3 = "Conservative." We did so because we wanted the "scores" to run from "least" to "most" conservative.

c. Now, you may recall from Exercise 12-8 that party identification (partisanship) colors how people see the world. It has also been found to have a strong connection with voting: party loyalists usually back their parties in elections. So perhaps the relationship you saw above (assuming that you think there is one) can be explained by the effects of party affiliation on those two variables. As the text indicates in Chapter 13, one way to find out is to control for partisanship by creating "subtables" based on the categories of the control variable. In other words, the previous cross-classification from which the chi-square, tau-b, and gamma were determined was a 3 × 4 table. To hold party identification constant we generated three such 3 × 4 tables, one for each level of party identification. (Reminder: for simplicity we are only considering the three major British parties.) Here are the results when we examined the attitude by vote relationship within the three categories of the control variable, party identification.

Subtable	"Level" of Party Identification	Chi- square	df	Tau-b	Gamma	N
1	Labour	16.992	8	−.04	−.11	919
2	Liberal Democrat	4.076	8	.03	.156	250
3	Conservative	47.347	8	.16	.41	566

Again, you might try replicating these findings by controlling for party identification (variable 01). In any event, try to interpret these results. Does the party variable explain or cancel the original relationship? (Tips: 1. Reread the section of Chapter 13 on multivariate analysis of categorical variables. 2. Compare each of the statistics in this table with the corresponding ones in the previous attitude by vote table. 3. Try calculating a [weighted] average of tau-b or gamma or both and then compare it to the measure in the two-way table above.)

Exercise 13-8. In this exercise, we will look at the effect of a third variable, REGION, on the relationship between senators' party identification (PARTYRD) and scores on the AFL-CIO scorecard (see Table 13-1). First, describe the relationship between PARTYRD and the AFL-CIO, which you can see by looking in the row labeled "Total." Then discuss how taking into account the region affects that relationship. Output using SPSS is provided below.

TABLE 13-1

Senators' Scores on AFL-CIO Scorecard by Party and Controlling for Region

Region	PARTYRD	Mean	N	Standard Deviation
1 Northeast	1 Democrat	74.4615	13	10.77509
	2 Republican	16.1429	7	23.61093
	Total	54.0500	20	32.61655
2 South	1 Democrat	60.8571	7	21.06679
	2 Republican	2.8571	14	5.68205
	Total	22.1905	21	30.64412
3 Midwest	1 Democrat	75.6000	10	7.53068
	2 Republican	10.5000	12	21.87776
	Total	40.0909	22	37.09179
4 West	1 Democrat	69.6667	9	12.42980
	2 Republican	1.8667	15	4.92612
	Total	27.2917	24	34.53603
Total	1 Democrat	71.2051	39	13.47938
	2 Republican	6.3958	48	15.10212
	Total	35.4483	87	35.43771

_____

_____

_____

_____

_____

_____

Exercise 13-9. Now take a look at the output, this time looking at the relationship between party and support for issues favored by the American Civil Liberties Union. In which region does the relationship between party and scorecard score the strongest? The weakest?

TABLE 13-2

Senators' Scores on American Civil Liberties Union Scorecard, by Party and Controlling for Region

Region	PARTYRD	Mean	N	Standard Deviation
1 Northeast	1 Democrat	55.0000	16	11.54701
	2 Republican	40.7143	7	19.24157
	Total	50.6522	23	15.39660
2 South	1 Democrat	56.6667	9	13.46291
	2 Republican	18.3333	15	7.71517
	Total	32.7083	24	21.41612
3 Midwest	1 Democrat	55.7143	14	11.57868
	2 Republican	28.3333	12	19.92410
	Total	43.0769	26	20.93212
4 West	1 Democrat	57.0000	10	6.74949
	2 Republican	24.6875	16	14.07939
	Total	37.1154	26	19.80773
Total	1 Democrat	55.9184	49	10.83366
	2 Republican	25.9000	50	16.21570
	Total	40.7576	99	20.40863

Exercise 13-10. Chapter 1 of *Political Science Research Methods* described a study that showed the deleterious effects of negative campaigning on voter turnout.[18] This important finding did not go unchallenged, however. In the spirit of replication that we discussed in Chapter 2, political scientists Martin Wattenberg and Craig Brians published an article that "directly contradict[s] their findings."[19] They rested their case partly on the analysis of two surveys, the "American National Election Study" for 1992 and 1996. The main independent variables were indicators of whether or not respondents remember hearing or seeing negative and positive political advertisements and if they made comments about these ads; that is, the variables were coded 1 if "yes, comments were made" and 0 if "no." The dependent variable was a dichotomy: Did the respondent vote or not? The researchers hypothesized that if being aware of attack ads does adversely affect citizenship, there should be a negative correlation between commenting on attack ads and voting. If, by contrast, exposure to such ads had little effect on potential voters, the relationship would be nil.

Besides these variables, they also included many other independent factors that might affect the decision to vote. Table 13-3 presents a small portion of their results for the 1996 survey respondents.[20]

a. The coefficients in the table constitute the terms of a logistic regression model. Write the model as an expression for the predicted probability of voting:

[18] Stephen D. Ansolabehere, Shanto Iyengar, and Adam Simon, "Replicating Experiments Using Aggregate and Survey Data: The Case of Negative Advertising and Turnout," *American Political Science Review* 93 (December 1999): 901–910.

[19] Martin P. Wattenberg and Craig Leonard Brians, "Negative Campaign Advertising: Demobilizer or Mobilizer," *American Political Science Review* 93 (December 1999): 891.

[20] Ibid., table 3, p. 894. Note that the Wattenberg and Brians model contains other control variables. We eliminated them just to keep things simple.

TABLE 13-3

Logistic Regression of Turnout on Advertising Recall and Other Variables

Variable	Partial Coefficient	Standard Error
Negative ad comment: 1 = yes, 0 = no	−.2005	.1792
Positive ad comment: 1 = yes, 0 = no	.2652	.2806
Newspaper political news index[a]	.0337	.0113
Age in years	.0295	.0054
Campaign interest: 1 = somewhat, 0 = otherwise	.3824	.1672
Campaign interest: 1 = very much, 0 = otherwise	2.0460	.3260
Gender: 1 = female, 0 = male	.3195	.1533
Time from interview to election (in days)	−.0053	.0043
Independent leaner:[b]		
1 = independents who lean toward a party, 0 = otherwise	.8183	.2647
Weak partisan:[b] 1 = weak partisan, 0 = all others	.7279	.2543
Strong partisan:[b] 1 = strong partisan, 0 = all others	1.7830	.2935
Race: 1 = white, 0 = nonwhite	.1962	.2057
Constant	−4.4223	.4223

N = 1,373. Percentage of respondents correctly predicted 81%, based on these variables plus others not in this table.

[a] Coded on scale from 0 to 28 with 28 being highest interest.
[b] Pure independent treated as reference category.

b.   Write the model as an expression for the estimated log odds (logit) of voting:

c. If someone had null (zero) values on all of the variables, what would his predicted probability of voting be? ————————————————————— (By the way, why do we write "his"?) What is the substantive interpretation of this probability? Does it make any sense?

———————————————————————————————

———————————————————————————————

———————————————————————————————

———————————————————————————————

———————————————————————————————

d. Now suppose a person is fifty years old but has null values on all the independent variables. Before doing any calculations look at the coefficient for age. Do you think this estimated probability would be higher than the previous one? Why?

———————————————————————————————

e. What is the predicted probability of voting for this fifty-year-old man? ——————— In words, what is the effect of age on the likelihood of voting when everything else is the same?

———————————————————————————————

———————————————————————————————

———————————————————————————————

f. Consider this same person. What are the estimated *log* odds that he will vote? ——————————————————. What are the estimated *odds* that the individual will go to the polls on election day? ——————————————— Give a commonsense interpretation of this latter estimate.

———————————————————————————————

———————————————————————————————

———————————————————————————————

g. Consider a sixty-year-old white female who is a strongly partisan Democrat, men-
    tioned both negative and positive commercials, has a score of 14 on the political
    news index, is very much interested in the campaign, and was interviewed five days
    before the election. What is the predicted probability that this person will vote? What
    are the odds of her voting? (Tip: List this woman's values on each of the variables.
    [That is, for instance, if she is "very interested" how would she be coded on that and
    the other interest variable?] Then substitute into the equation for the predicted
    probability.)

    _____

    _____

    _____

    _____

    _____

h. Compare the above person with an identical male. Who is more likely to vote? Why?

    _____

    _____

    _____

    _____

    _____

i. Which of the coefficients in the table are significant?

    _____

    _____

    _____

    _____

    _____

j. In your view are the authors correct in saying that exposure to negative political commercials does not depress turnout? (Tip: Think about the main independent variable. Then consider a "typical" person, as we did in some of the previous questions. Get the estimated probability or odds of voting for this individual both when he or she mentions negative ads [that is, when the score is "1"] and when no negative commercials are mentioned. How much do the probabilities or odds change?)

_____

_____

_____

_____

_____

Exercise 13-11. This is a tricky assignment, but one that resembles a lot of actual political and social research. The term "white flight" has been used to describe demographic change in urban America since at least the 1960s. Using the city data mentioned above, try to build an explanatory model of the change in the white population in central cities from 1980 to 1990. (There are two versions, "stateofcities.dat" and "stateofcities.por," a portable SPSS file.) That is, treat "percent change in white population from 1980 to 1990" as the dependent variable and attempt to explain variation in change with indicators from various categories of possible explanatory factors. For instance, you hypothesize (ahead of time!) that crime, poor housing, increased minority density, pollution and congestion, declining city services, and loss of job opportunities are at least associated with the changing demographic composition of cities. Report your results in a form acceptable to your instructor.

Exercise 13-12. Instead of "white flight," identify a different variable that might be interesting to analyze.

Exercise 13-13. The CD-ROM contains several other files of various types. Pick an issue or problem in political science or politics and see if there are data that might lend themselves to its analysis. You can use the procedure mentioned above to organize your thinking, even if the data are strictly nominal or ordinal.